Peremptory International Legal Norms and the Democratic Rule of Law

Peremptory International Legal Norms and the Democratic Rule of Law explores the risks to the democratic State inherent in the attempt to divorce the notion of democratic rule of law from respect for and adherence to peremptory international legal norms which allow for no derogation therefrom such as the prohibition of torture and inhumane treatment or punishment by the State.

The chapters address, with specific current case examples, in what ways the democratic rule of law within certain democratic States risk being undermined through those States acquiescing to the erosion of peremptory international law norms in the domestic and international context. The book therefore explores the question of in what ways such democratic State acquiescence in effect may ultimately disrupt the investment within the State in the shared culture of core human rights values that underlies democratic rule of law itself and highlights the fragility of that shared culture. The contributors argue for a renewed commitment in principle and practice to the democratic rule of law and to its human rights international normative underpinnings.

Peremptory International Legal Norms and the Democratic Rule of Law will be of great interest to scholars of international law, human rights and democracy. The chapters originally published as a special issue of *The International Journal of Human Rights.*

Sonja Grover is a Professor with Lakehead University and an Associate Editor of *The International Journal of Human Rights* who has published extensively in the field of international law including a previous edited volume with Routledge entitled *The Responsibility to Protect: Perspectives on the Concept's Meaning, Proper Application and Value.*

Peremptory International Legal Norms and the Democratic Rule of Law

Edited by
Sonja Grover

Routledge
Taylor & Francis Group
LONDON AND NEW YORK

First published 2020
by Routledge
2 Park Square, Milton Park, Abingdon, Oxon, OX14 4RN

and by Routledge
52 Vanderbilt Avenue, New York, NY 10017

Routledge is an imprint of the Taylor & Francis Group, an informa business

First issued in paperback 2021

British Library Cataloguing in Publication Data
A catalogue record for this book is available from the British Library

ISBN13: 978-0-367-41989-9 (hbk)
ISBN13: 978-1-03-208406-0 (pbk)

Typeset in Minion Pro
by Newgen Publishing UK

Publisher's Note
The publisher accepts responsibility for any inconsistencies that may have arisen during the conversion of this book from journal articles to book chapters, namely the inclusion of journal terminology.

Disclaimer
Every effort has been made to contact copyright holders for their permission to reprint material in this book. The publishers would be grateful to hear from any copyright holder who is not here acknowledged and will undertake to rectify any errors or omissions in future editions of this book.

Contents

Citation Information

The chapters in this book were originally published in *The International Journal of Human Rights FJHR*, volume 22, issue 10 (December 2018). When citing this material, please use the original page numbering for each article, as follows:

Introduction

Sonja Grover
The International Journal of Human Rights FJHR, volume 22, issue 10 (December 2018), pp. 1267–1268.

Chapter 1

International order, the rule of law, and US departures from refugee protection
Alise Coen
The International Journal of Human Rights FJHR, volume 22, issue 10 (December 2018), pp. 1269–1284.

Chapter 2

The harbinger theory of terrorism and the rule of law: the danger of 'balancing' non-derogable rights against security when relying on threat assessments produced by self-interested intelligence agencies
Ryan Alford
The International Journal of Human Rights FJHR, volume 22, issue 10 (December 2018), pp. 1285–1301.

Chapter 3

Citizenship by descent: how Canada's one-generation rule fails to comply with international legal norms
Mariette Brennan and Miriam Cohen
The International Journal of Human Rights FJHR, volume 22, issue 10 (December 2018), pp. 1302–1317.

Chapter 4

Securitisation, non-refoulement *and the rule of law in Kenya: the case of Somali refugees*
Oscar Gakuo Mwangi
The International Journal of Human Rights FJHR, volume 22, issue 10 (December 2018), pp. 1318–1334.

Chapter 5

The widespread use of torture in Mexico and its impacts on the rule of law
Denise González-Núñez
The International Journal of Human Rights FJHR, volume 22, issue 10 (December 2018), pp. 1335–1354.

Chapter 6

EU membership conditionality in promoting acceptance of peremptory human rights norms: a case study in Albania considering public opinion
Ridvan Peshkopia, Drin Konjufca, Erblin Salihu and Jonida Lika
The International Journal of Human Rights FJHR, volume 22, issue 10 (December 2018), pp. 1355–1376.

Notes on Contributors

Ryan Alford is an Associate Professor at Bora Laskin Faculty of Law and a visiting fellow at the Max Planck Institute for European Legal History in 2019. He is the author of *Permanent State of Emergency: Unchecked Executive Power and the Demise of the Rule of Law* (2017), and is currently writing a book entitled *What Does Canada's Rule of Law Protect? Recovering the Rights Protected by Our Unwritten Constitutional Principles.*

Mariette Brennan is an Associate Professor at the Bora Laskin Faculty of Law at Lakehead University. She holds a PhD (Law) from Osgoode Hall Law School, York University, an LLM (with distinction) in International Human Rights Law from the University of Essex (United Kingdom) and a JD from the University of Ottawa. Her main areas of research are constitutional and public health law.

Alise Coen received her PhD from the University of Delaware in Political Science and International Relations. She is currently Assistant Professor of Political Science at the University of Wisconsin-Sheboygan. Her research explores connections among global governance, humanitarian displacement crises, international human rights norms and US foreign policy. Her work has appeared in *Ethics & International Affairs*, *Politics and Religion*, *Global Change, Peace & Security* and *The International Journal of Human Rights.*

Miriam Cohen is an Assistant Professor of International Law at the Faculty of Law, University of Montreal. Her teaching and research focus is on international human rights, international criminal law and victims' rights. She is currently conducting research on reparations for international crimes and human rights violations funded by a prestigious SSHRC Insight Development grant.

Denise González-Núñez is Director of the Human Rights Program at Universidad Iberoamericana, Mexico City, an office dedicated to carrying out research and advocacy to advance human rights in Mexico. She holds a Master of Studies in International Human Rights Law from the University of Oxford and her research interests include human rights law and public policy, grave human rights violations, refugee law and land rights, among others.

Drin Konjufca is a graduate student with the University for Business and Technology, Kosovo. His research interests cover international relations and comparative politics. He has presented papers in several international conferences.

Jonida Lika received an MA in Sociology from the University of Tirana, Albania. Her research interests cover social theory, European Union politics and public opinion data gathering. She has presented papers at several national and international conferences.

Oscar Gakuo Mwangi is Associate Professor of Political Science and Head of the Department of Political and Administrative Studies, National University of Lesotho. His research interests are in comparative politics, especially in the areas of democratisation and governance, conflict and security, and environmental politics in eastern and southern Africa. His teaching areas are in the fields of comparative politics, international relations and political theory.

Ridvan Peshkopia teaches Political Science at the University for Business and Technology, Kosovo. His research interests cover international relations, political behaviour, EU eastward enlargement, institutional reforms, intergroup relations, public opinion and migration studies. His publications have appeared in *Journal of Behavioral and Social Sciences*, *Punishment & Society*, *Policy Futures in Education* and *Framework: A Journal of Cinema and the Media*. His most recent book is *Conditioning Democratization: Institutional Reforms and EU membership Conditionality in Albania and Macedonia* (2014).

Erblin Salihu is a graduate student from the University for Business and Technology, Kosovo. His research interests cover international relations and public opinion. He has presented papers at several international conferences.

Introduction

Sonja Grover

This special issue explores the risks to the democratic State inherent in the attempt to divorce the notion of the democratic rule of law from respect for and adherence to peremptory international legal norms (customary and *jus cogens* law) that set out various of the most fundamental human rights including but not limited to the right to respect for one's human dignity and security of the person psychologically and physically. The papers address with specific case examples in what ways the democratic rule of law within certain democratic States risks being undermined through those States acquiescing in a particular way(s) to the erosion of certain international customary or *jus cogens* norms in the domestic and/or international context. The special issue addresses the question then of in what way such democratic State acquiescence in effect ultimately may disrupt the investment within the State in the shared culture of core human rights values that underlie the democratic rule of law itself and highlights the fragility of that shared culture. The special issue papers thus in sum argue for a renewed commitment in principle and practice to the democratic rule of law and to its human rights international normative underpinnings.

In her paper *International order, the rule of law, and U.S. departures from refugee protection* Alise Coen argues that 'international human rights norms and respect for the rule of law are mutually sustaining pillars of a liberal international order' and that 'State behaviors undermining customary and *jus cogens* legal norms are exceptionally disruptive to possibilities of global justice'. Coen advances the notion that '*non-refoulement* and a Responsibility to Protect refugees are connected to universally binding and peremptory norms in important ways such that state violations of these principles undermine the premises of international legal order'. She explores within that frame certain U.S. refugee policies under the Trump administration and their implications in her view for democratic rule of law.

Ryan Alford's paper is titled *The harbinger theory of terrorism and the rule of law: The danger of 'balancing' non-derogable rights against security when relying on threat assessments produced by self-interested intelligence agencies.* Alford explores some problematic examples of how Canada's security apparatus (which he holds has an inherent conflict of interest that may affect threat assessments) has addressed the threat to the Global North of mass terror attacks. He explores what he argues are the inevitable improper adverse implications for democratic rule of law of balancing non-derogable rights against State security. Alford contends that in fact the 'new framework of "balancing" rights against security entails a repudiation of the concept of non-derogability in practice' a cornerstone of international human rights and refugee law.

Mariette Brennan and Miriam Cohen are the co-authors of *Citizenship by Descent: How Canada's One-Generation Rule Fails to Comply with International Legal Norms*. Brennan and Cohen explore how changes to Canada's rules regarding citizenship by descent (namely 'denying second and subsequent generations of Canadians born abroad the right to citizenship by descent') likely would render some children stateless 'thus violating international law and the rule of law'. Brennan and Cohen argue that Canada must introduce legal reforms to its citizenship by descent laws to ensure such laws do not contribute to statelessness and better ensure that crafting of any new laws on citizenship carefully consider the issue of statelessness lest individual basic human rights be undermined by exacerbating the problem of statelessness.

Oscar Gakuo Mwangi's paper *Securitisation, non-refoulement and the rule of law in Kenya: the case of Somali refugees* explores what he maintains are violations of Kenyan domestic and of international law through the improper refoulement of Somali refugees in Kenya. That refoulement occurring under the false justification of securitisation and *blanket* characterisation of the Somali refugees as terrorists. His paper explores the possible role of non-state actors in challenging false blanket narratives about particular refugee groups.

Denise González-Núñez's paper is titled *The widespread use of torture in Mexico and its impacts on the rule of law*. González-Núñez's outlines the scope of the persistent problem in Mexico of the use of 'torture ... in various contexts, its use in criminal proceedings, [and] as an "illegal" method of criminal investigation to obtain confessions and incriminating statements'. She argues that the relatively unfettered use of torture in various aspects of criminal law enforcement and prosecutorial procedure in Mexico 'has translated in an almost absolute incapacity to enforce the law according to human rights standards' thus eroding the very notion of democratic rule of law.

The paper *EU Membership Conditionality in Promoting Acceptance of Peremptory Human Rights Norms: A Case Study in Albania Considering Public Opinion* authored by Ridvan Peshkopia, Drin Konjufca, Erblin Salihu and Jonida Lika explores a disconnect in certain instances in public opinion regarding on the one hand support for EU membership and such membership conditionality as an agent of democratisation in the country and, on the other, views about what constitute basic *jus cogens* human rights. The authors report a case study on this issue conducted using 2016 public opinion survey data collected in Albania. That data reveal that EU membership being conditioned on promoting and protecting human rights in the State in question is not consistently sufficient to promote among the populace widespread support for all EU -stipulated basic human rights.

Disclosure statement

No potential conflict of interest was reported by the author.

International order, the rule of law, and US departures from refugee protection

Alise Coen

ABSTRACT

Compliance with international human rights norms and respect for the rule of law are mutually sustaining pillars of a liberal international order. State behaviours undermining customary and *jus cogens* legal norms are exceptionally disruptive to possibilities of global justice. This article posits that *non-refoulement* and a responsibility to protect refugees are connected to universally binding and peremptory norms in important ways such that state violations of these principles undermine the premises of international legal order. The article focuses on US norm violations in these areas, contextualising policy changes under the Trump administration within previous US departures from refugee protection principles. Given the position of the United States as a hegemonic and democratic actor in the international system, the article argues that US actions contra non-refoulement and efforts to shirk refugee responsibility-sharing in the wake of *jus cogens* crimes are particularly damaging to the foundations of global human rights governance and attendant notions of legitimacy and the rule of law.

Introduction

Diverse perspectives within International Relations (IR) theory have converged around the notion that the global architecture underpinning the contemporary world order is at a crossroads.[1] At the heart of this juncture is the crisis of a distinctly liberal international order built on a rules-based system of multilateralism, democratic solidarity and human rights.[2] There are robust foundations for connecting norm-violating behaviour to this crisis and its attendant erosions of the rule of law at both domestic and international levels. Much work has focused on the rule of law as a state-level attribute, demonstrating the centrality of fair, impartial and effective institutions for democratic political systems.[3] Applied to the international domain, the rule of law anticipates that states and other actors will adhere to a wide range of principles prescribed by legal norms to ensure a sense of fairness, procedural transparency and predictability.[4] Violations of customary and peremptory legal norms – universally binding norms of a *jus cogens* nature from which no derogations are permitted – can cripple the expectations associated with these components of international order and justice. Deviations from human rights principles are particularly problematic since the rule of law depends on equally enforced laws 'consistent with international human rights norms and standards'.[5]

The responsibility for adhering to these principles arguably rests first and foremost with powerful states that possess the governance capacity to comply with them, as weaker states sometimes lack the durable administrative institutions needed to enforce human rights laws within their territories.[6] Strong states espousing a liberal democratic identity are particularly integral to sustaining the normative and legal power of international human rights instruments since they possess both material and ideational conditions supportive of human rights compliance. What, then, are the implications for global human rights governance when a democratic, hegemonic actor violates core human rights principles? This article focuses on US norm violations in the realm of refugee protection to explore this question. Violations of the principle of *non-refoulement* and efforts to shirk refugee responsibility-sharing in the wake of mass atrocity crimes are highlighted as two important realms in which US behaviours undermine the rule of law and weaken international order.

The article proceeds in four parts. The first section provides an overview of salient connections between international order and the rule of law, defining these concepts and highlighting their intertwinement with human rights norms. The second section discusses core human rights principles manifest in two realms of refugee protection that bear important connections to *jus cogens* and customary legal norms: the obligations of non-refoulement and a responsibility to protect refugees fleeing mass atrocity crimes. The third section of the article explores US norm violations in these and other relevant areas, contextualising policy changes during the first year of the Trump administration within previous US departures from refugee protection principles. The article concludes with a consideration of the consequences of these norm violations for notions of legitimacy, the rule of law and international order.

International order and the rule of law

Member states at the United Nations (UN) World Summit in 2005 committed to 'actively protecting and promoting all human rights, the rule of law and democracy', recognising the 'interlinked and mutually reinforcing' nature of these concepts.[7] At the international level, the rule of law provides an important sense of stability and predictability in the absence of a centralised world polity. While definitions of the concept vary, the rule of law might be conceptualised as entailing four main principles: governments and other actors are accountable under the law; laws are just and applied evenly, and protect fundamental rights; the processes by which laws are enacted and enforced are accessible and fair; and the delivery of justice is competent and ethical.[8] Accountability under the law and the equal enforcement of laws protecting basic human rights are particularly central in enabling states and other actors to maintain standards of fair behaviour. When states fail to comply with their legal commitments and uphold fundamental human rights protections, the principles of accountability, fairness and equal enforcement underpinning the rule of law are undermined. Moreover, because the efficacy of international law depends on its successful internalisation and enforcement among states, widespread violations of international standards can precipitate a breakdown in global justice.[9]

Encroachments on the international rule of law simultaneously encroach on international order. International order encompasses 'the body of rules, norms, and institutions that govern relations among the key players in the international environment'.[10] Contemporary international order depends particularly on adherence to liberal political norms upholding human rights. Noncompliance with such norms is often understood as endangering human rights and international stability writ large.[11] For democracies, human rights violations can jeopardise the rule of law and notions of legitimacy at domestic and international levels. States' adherence to human rights norms represents an important signalling of their commitment to democracy[12] as well as their membership in a club of nations that adhere to 'laws of universal conscience'.[13] Expectations that democracies fulfil their moral commitments under international law have intensified as notions of international order have increasingly linked democracy with human rights.[14] Compliance with human rights norms has become paramount to shared understandings of global governance, justice and accountability, such that states are increasingly willing to prioritise commitments to international human rights law over short-term material interests, even at significant economic costs.[15]

When such norms have acquired peremptory or *jus cogens* status, they are especially foundational to preserving the rule of law on which international order depends. *Jus cogens* status signals acceptance by the international community of states as a whole, and states cannot derogate from or opt out of *jus cogens* obligations, even by treaty.[16] Greater attention to the connection between *jus cogens* norms and international order is needed within IR, as these binding international standards are arguably central to the ethos of the international community. Conklin posits that violations of these norms call into question the very existence of the international legal order, for 'when a state contravenes the peremptory norm, the legitimacy/authority of the international community in which the preemptory norm is nested is annulled'.[17] Widely accepted examples of *jus cogens* norms include prohibitions against attacks on civilians, genocide and torture.[18] Such prohibitions represent the extent to which core values of the international community surrounding human rights have become 'so fundamental to the system that the law could not survive without them'.[19]

Core human rights principles and refugee protection

International human rights law provides a fundamental basis for the protection of asylum-seekers, refugees and forcibly displaced persons by shielding these individuals from violations of accepted international norms.[20] This section of the article outlines two areas of refugee protection that merit attention: the principle of non-refoulement and the responsibility to protect refugees fleeing mass atrocity crimes. Because these realms might be considered intrinsically connected to peremptory human rights norms of a *jus cogens* nature and to customary international human rights law, state violations of these obligations simultaneously undermine the rule of law, democratic legitimacy and international order.

Non-refoulement

In exploring the emergence of the right to asylum as a customary norm in international law, much attention has been paid to Article 33 in the 1951 Convention on the Status of Refugees (Refugee Convention) and its provisions for non-refoulement – provisions prohibiting states from expelling or returning individuals to territories where they might face persecution or torture. In addition to prohibiting states from returning individuals to territories where their lives or freedom may be threatened, the principle holds that refugees and asylum-seekers cannot be prevented from pursuing protection once they have come under a state's jurisdiction, regardless of whether their entry and presence in the state is lawful.[21] The prohibition on refoulement is widely acknowledged as binding international customary law in the sense that all states, regardless of whether they are party to refugee conventions, are expected to adhere to the principle.[22]

As the cornerstone of refugee protection, many scholars have argued that non-refoulement additionally rises to the status of a peremptory or *jus cogens* norm from which no derogation is permitted.[23] Its peremptory status has been affirmed by the United Nations High Commissioner for Refugees (UNHCR),[24] and references to non-refoulement as '*jus cogens*' are also found in regional instruments such as the Cartagena Declaration and the Brazil Declaration.[25] Non-refoulement is fundamental to the *jus cogens* prohibition on torture and cruel, inhuman or degrading treatment in the event that returning or deporting individuals to a territory might subject them to such treatment.[26] Components of the European Convention on Human Rights (ECHR), the International Covenant on Civil and Political Rights (ICCPR) and the Convention against Torture (CAT) have all been cited as evidence that the obligations of non-refoulement are binding and non-derogable.[27] In considering its *jus cogens* status, Da Lomba notes that 'no state has ever overtly contested the binding nature of the principle of non-refoulement during debates at the UN General Assembly, including States that are not party to the 1951 Convention and/or the 1967 Protocol'.[28]

A strong case can therefore be made for non-refoulement as a peremptory norm. It is important to note, however, that national security and public safety exceptions provided for in the Refugee Convention might enable states to derogate from the principle under certain circumstances. The UNHCR specifies such exceptions to be conditional on 'strict compliance with due process of law' and emphasises that 'all reasonable steps must first be taken to secure the admission of the individual concerned to a safe third country'.[29] While the parameters for lawful exceptions are quite limited, Duffy argues that the practices of states regarding 'terrorist exceptions' in the post-September 11 environment have hindered the principle's peremptory status.[30] Non-refoulement is thus characterised by some, given its contested status, as an 'emerging' or 'evolving' *jus cogens* norm.[31] It is grounded firmly in treaties, international human rights and refugee law, and in customary international law.[32]

A responsibility to protect refugees fleeing mass atrocities

The normative framework of the Responsibility to Protect (R2P) is also relevant to *jus cogens* obligations underpinning international order and the rule of law. In addition to recommitting themselves to human rights and the rule of law, UN member states at the 2005 World Summit accepted a collective responsibility to protect populations from genocide, war crimes, ethnic cleansing and crimes against humanity, using 'appropriate diplomatic, humanitarian and other peaceful means'.[33] R2P was reaffirmed by the UN Security Council in 2014 with the adoption of Resolution 2150,[34] though its mainstreaming has been hindered by continued reservations about potentially intrusive measures of implementation.[35] While contestation centres on its coercive elements and conflation with humanitarian intervention, a nascent body of work has connected R2P explicitly to a responsibility to protect refugees fleeing mass atrocity crimes – emphasising non-coercive measures such as the provision of asylum, resettlement and upholding of non-refoulement as important policy tools for protecting civilians from grave human rights abuses.[36]

There are clear links between R2P as a human rights framework and peremptory norms in international law. Primarily, the four mass atrocity crimes triggering its applicability are generally recognised as *jus cogens* crimes.[37] Moreover, Glanville observes the nexus between R2P and *jus cogens* norms in Article 41(1) of the draft International Law Commission (ILC) articles on the 'Responsibility of States for Internationally Wrongful Acts', which calls on states to collectively cooperate to address and counteract the effects of 'any serious breaches' of the peremptory norms of international law.[38] While the ILC articles do not specify a precise form for state cooperation, refugee responsibility-sharing in the face of mass displacement caused by breaches of *jus cogens* norms arguably represents one important duty of the international community in this regard. Scholars of genocide and mass killing note that barriers to immigration for victims fleeing violence and inadequate refugee responsibility-sharing among states have enabled substantially higher death tolls in mass atrocity situations.[39] Fulfilling a responsibility to protect refugees fleeing grave human rights abuses is therefore integral to preventing further victimisation in the wake of *jus cogens* crimes.

While neither R2P nor the international refugee regime provides clear mechanisms for allocating responsibilities, attention has been paid to the relative capacities of states to offer asylum and other forms of protection for refugees, measured by factors like economic development, unemployment level, population density and territorial size.[40] Recent European Union proposals for distributing asylum-seekers among member states have similarly focused on capability-related factors like national population and wealth levels.[41] Studies have also proposed focusing on culpability, integrating the impact of past policy decisions by major powers more centrally into refugee responsibility-sharing schemes. This work highlights special duties and obligations stemming from military interventions, support for oppressive regimes and other foreign policy actions contributing to mass displacement crises.[42] Precise formulas for allocating responsibilities to protect refugees remain contested, but it is reasonable to conclude that states with strong capacities to offer asylum and other forms of protection for victims fleeing mass atrocity crimes should fulfil their obligations to do so as members of the international community, even if they were not culpable in creating the conditions that facilitated grave human rights abuses. For major powers possessing both a capacity to absorb refugees and culpability-based responsibilities connected to *jus cogens* crimes, the duty to offer refugee protections to certain groups of displacees might be doubly strong.

Norm violations by the United States

As a global superpower, the United States is in a unique position to bolster equitable and effective global governance and affirm core human rights norms undergirding the international rule of law. Ikenberry casts the foundations of a liberal international order built around rules-based relations as dependent on US hegemony and links the contemporary crisis in this world order to a crisis of US leadership and authority.[43] For decades, the convergence of its material capabilities and identity as a liberal democracy prompted the United States to pursue democracy and human rights promotion abroad as a means of establishing and imposing its legitimacy and expertise.[44] When the United States violates peremptory and customary human rights norms, it compromises its legitimacy and also carves out important precedents for less powerful states to follow suit with the understanding that a hegemonic actor has implicitly endorsed such deviations in its own behaviours, undermining the foundations of the international rule of law. As Sikkink observes, 'the real test of international law and [human rights] norms is their ability to influence the actions of even the most powerful states'.[45] A consideration of US behaviour is therefore paramount for grappling with human rights norms compliance and its implications for international order.

This section explores US violations of core human rights principles in the realm of refugee protection. Policies enacted during the first year of the Trump administration indicate significant breaks with customary and peremptory norms regarding protections for refugees and asylum-seekers and further erode principles of non-discrimination that underpin the democratic rule of law. Before exploring those policies, it is beneficial to briefly probe how contemporary US violations have emerged in a context of previous deviations from commitments to international refugee law.

US departures from refugee protection principles

In ratifying the 1967 Protocol relating to the Status of Refugees, the United States bound itself to the international refugee regime and to the protections enshrined in Articles 2 through 34 of the Refugee Convention. These include the definition of a refugee, the treatment of refugees and the prohibition on returning persons to destinations where they might face harm or persecution (i.e. non-refoulement).[46] The Refugee Act of 1980 was intended to bring US asylum policy in line with international legal standards. However, both policymakers and the courts have enabled US refugee policy to violate international norms even when international standards are clear and peremptory.[47] One prominent example of US manoeuvring to circumvent non-refoulement includes the interception of boats of Haitian asylum-seekers in the early 1990s to prevent them from arriving directly on US territory. Over 65,000 individuals were interdicted and immediately returned to Haiti by the US Coast Guard without any evaluation of asylum claims.[48] The US Supreme Court and members of Congress upheld the validity of the Haitian interdiction programme in 1993, interpreting the prohibition on non-refoulement to apply only to refugees already within the territorial borders of contracting states.[49] This interpretation was substantially at odds with international standards and stands out as an early US departure from refugee protection norms in the post-Cold War environment. It is noteworthy that the violation of non-refoulement vis-à-vis Haitian asylum-seekers occurred amidst a growing nativist wave in US politics framing the influx of Mexican, Latino, Haitian and other migrants of colour within discourses of 'invasion', 'hyperfertility', 'criminals' and 'welfare-takers'.[50] This suggests an important connection between international human rights norm violations and domestic erosions of non-discrimination principles intrinsic to the democratic rule of law.

Violations of basic human rights and international refugee law have repeatedly manifested in the US treatment of asylum-seekers along its southern border. These include evidence of long and arbitrary periods of detention, pressures to withdraw asylum claims, and lack of access to due process and legal representation rights.[51] The UNHCR's 2016 report expressed particular concern over the continued US detention of vulnerable groups such as child asylum-seekers, the lack of access to legal advice for detained asylum-seekers, and contracts with private prison corporations and local jails that result in asylum-seekers in the United States being detained in the same locations and conditions as suspected or convicted criminals.[52] Such treatment violates important international human rights standards, including protections against detention and restrictions on the freedom of movement under the CAT, the ICCPR, the Refugee Convention and regional instruments.[53] The Refugee Convention, for example, requires states to treat asylum-seekers as presumptive refugees, affording them the right to freedom of movement and avoiding their detention unless exceptional circumstances necessitate it according to a narrow set of objectives.[54] Moreover, 'protection is owed to a person meeting the definition (whether or not status has been formally assessed) who is under a State party's jurisdiction … and immigration penalties may not be imposed for unlawful entry or presence dictated by flight from persecution'.[55]

Despite extreme conditions of human tragedy characterising the threats faced by asylum-seekers from Central America,[56] these groups have been politicised and securitised along with asylum-seekers from Mexico through the prism of an 'illegal immigration crisis' in US politics. Nativist narratives emphasising an 'immigration invasion'[57] have provided local-level justifications for violating international human rights law and resonate within a long history of casting black and Latino identity outside the parameters of American national belonging, as 'unfit neighbours and suspect citizens'.[58] Elements of nativism and racial discrimination at work in both the Haitian interdiction programme and the internment and deportation of asylum-seekers along the southern US border raise concerns for the democratic rule of law. Nondiscrimination and equality are salient values in liberal democracies and essential elements underpinning the rule of law.[59] Moreover, protecting the rights, equality and dignity not only of citizens but also of foreigners is integral to a truly *democratic* rule of law.[60]

US behaviour in this area has violated important human rights norms regarding non-internment and non-discrimination, whereby 'one ought not to be subjected to detention without charge or trial on the basis of ascribed or acquired characteristics (such as race, religion, or nationality)'.[61] Concerns regarding US violations of non-discrimination in the treatment of asylum-seekers have intensified since the September 11 attacks. Studies show an increase in the denial of asylum claims for individuals from Arabic-speaking countries and evidence of growing discrimination based on language heritage skills among both US asylum officers and immigration judges.[62] A significant departure from non-discrimination principles occurred with the commencement of Operation Liberty Shield in 2003, a programme initiated within the US Department of Homeland Security. In addition to heightening security measures at borders and airports, the programme modified asylum procedures by requiring the detention of asylum-seekers from over 30 countries where 'al-Qaeda, al-Qaeda sympathizers, and other terrorist groups are known to have operated'.[63] The initiative mandated that even asylum-seekers who raised no security suspicions be detained for the duration of their asylum proceedings – typically lasting well over six months – on the basis of their national origin.[64]

Departures from refugee protection principles continued with the Real ID Act, passed by the US Congress and signed into law by President Bush in 2005. Its changes to the asylum process were framed in terms of protecting Americans from the threat of terrorists seeking entry by posing as refugees or asylum-seekers. This legislation amended the US Immigration and Naturalization Act (INA) to add new requirements to the burden of proof placed on asylum applicants, including requiring proof that one of the statutory grounds for refugee status (race, religion, nationality, membership in a particular social group, or political opinion) was the *central motive* for persecution rather than one of several mixed motives. The legislation also allowed for the denial of a petition for asylum if even minor inaccuracies were found in an asylum-seeker's statements, regardless of whether the inconsistencies were centrally relevant to the applicant's claim.[65]

Trump-era violations

As previously discussed, the Refugee Convention allows for the removal and denial of refugee status to individuals who have committed serious crimes and pose a danger to public safety when there are 'reasonable grounds' for establishing this danger. The high standards for determining that a refugee or asylum-seeker is a serious criminal and threat to the host country are intended to ensure states deny or expel only 'truly dangerous refugees'.[66] Deviations from refugee protection principles during the first year of the Trump administration arguably fail to meet these standards, and perpetuate violations of non-discrimination detrimental to the democratic rule of law. At the centre of controversial US policy changes were heightened efforts to limit and restrict refugees' right of entry in the January 2017 'Executive Order Protecting the Nation from Foreign Terrorist Entry into the United States'. This order imposed a temporary ban on the entry of all immigrant and non-immigrant nationals from seven Middle Eastern and North African countries and specified an indefinite ban on the entry of all Syrian refugees.[67]

The executive action arguably violated customary and peremptory legal norms in two ways. First, the policy undermined the prohibition on non-refoulement. In considering aspects of the principle that rise to the level of *jus cogens*, Goodwin-Gill notes that in addition to the obligation not to deny asylum-seekers and refugees access to international protection, 'there is a corresponding obligation on states not to frustrate the exercise of the right of asylum in such a way as to leave individuals at risk of persecution or other relevant harm'.[68] Reports on the detention and expulsion of individuals arriving in US airports in the aftermath of the executive order indicate the United States contravened non-refoulement in failing to uphold the procedural requirement for anyone in US custody or territory – including US airport detention – to be given a fair opportunity to claim credible fear of torture or persecution.[69] The US ratification of the CAT obligates asylum officers to provide 'credible fear of torture' screenings to determine whether asylum eligibility exists,[70] reiterating the nexus between non-refoulement and the *jus cogens* prohibition on torture.

Second, in denying and frustrating the right of Syrian refugees in particular to seek asylum, the executive action undermined the responsibility to protect refugees fleeing *jus cogens* crimes. Given that Syrian refugees are fleeing war crimes, acts of genocide and crimes against humanity,[71] impeding their escape might violate peremptory norms regarding prohibitions on these severe crimes. As part of a legal obligation to prevent genocide, which is clearly recognised as *jus cogens*,[72] states arguably have a duty to offer asylum and other forms of protection to individuals fleeing acts of genocide or violent contexts that may expose them to a future risk of genocide if they are unable to find safety. The same holds in the case of individuals seeking escape from war crimes and crimes against humanity since these are also often recognised as *jus cogens* crimes subject to universal jurisdiction.[73] The administration's targeting of Syrian refugees for denial of entry is thus particularly problematic in terms of US compliance with peremptory norms.

It is also important to note that the executive order breached non-discrimination requirements regarding the application of Article 33 of the Refugee Convention as well as article 26 of the ICCPR by utilising 'sweeping group-based denial of access to protection'.[74] Following a series of injunctions from US Federal district judges raising concerns about its discriminatory basis – specifically, its disproportionate impact on largely Arab and Muslim immigrants – the policy was modified to incorporate two non-Muslim majority countries: North Korea and Venezuela. Concerns regarding discrimination continued, however, given that the revised version only banned certain Venezuelan government officials and their immediate family members and had little impact on already low levels of immigration from North Korea. Nationals from Muslim-majority countries like Syria, Chad, Yemen, Libya and Iran continued to face large-scale immigrant and non-immigrant entry suspensions.[75] The disproportionate impact on Arab and Muslim migrants not only suggests a US violation of international human rights law vis-à-vis non-discrimination,[76] but also indicates further damage to the tenets of equality and non-discrimination foundational to the democratic rule of law at the domestic level.

The containment of refugee flows and measures such as border closures have the potential to undermine the fundamental right to leave and seek asylum.[77] Efforts to block asylum during the first year of the Trump administration resulted in a 37% decrease in total refugee admissions for fiscal year 2017, with the overall admissions figure (53,716) representing the lowest level of US refugee resettlement in 10 years.[78] The effect of the administration's attempts to restrict asylum for Syrian refugees in particular is evidenced in their dramatic admission declines. Whereas an average of 1200 Syrian refugees per month were admitted in the final months of the Obama administration, that figure fell below 285 per month during the spring of 2017. In August of 2017, as the number of Syrian refugees registered with the UN reached a record global high of 5.2 million, only 48 were admitted into the United States. Despite court injunctions and domestic legal challenges to its executive actions on immigration, the Trump administration was ultimately successful in curtailing the total annual admission of Syrian refugees by nearly half (6557 down from 12,587).[79]

In the fall of 2017, the US administration announced it would further reduce total refugee admissions to no more than 45,000 for 2018, representing the lowest annual ceiling since the establishment of the US refugee resettlement programme in 1980.[80] In terms of international refugee responsibility-sharing, these figures translate to a commitment from the global hegemon to accept only 0.2 percent of the world's 22.5 million refugees. The indifference to a responsibility to protect refugees fleeing mass atrocity crimes such as those in Syria is striking not only given the United States' relatively strong capacity to absorb refugees, but also given its culpability in contributing to the conditions shaping humanitarian displacement in Syria.[81] The implications for the resettlement of Syrian and other refugees originating from the Middle East and from Muslim-majority polities may be especially dire in the wake of new vetting policies requiring additional security screening and scrutinising of applications for refugees from 11 countries deemed to be 'higher risk' by the administration. These were reported to include Egypt, Iran, Iraq, Libya, Mali, North Korea, Somalia, South Sudan, Sudan, Syria and Yemen.[82] Refugee advocates cautioned that the effect of this additional 'vetting' during 2018 would likely pause the security checks and processing of refugees from these states, further slowing already backlogged security advisory opinions and resulting in a 'de facto ban' on refugees from these countries.[83] It is noteworthy that the conflicts driving displacement in several of the listed states are characterised by mass atrocity crimes, including acts of genocide and crimes against humanity such as widespread torture. This reiterates the potential for US policy to violate *jus cogens* and customary legal norms.

Violations of non-refoulement during the first year of the Trump administration extend beyond the controversial executive order to encompass wider accounts of increased detention and deportation of asylum-seekers.[84] In addition to undermining the international rule of law, changes in the practices of US Customs and Border Protection (CBP) under the Trump administration arguably compromise the domestic rule of law. A 2017 class-action lawsuit on behalf of asylum-seekers from Mexico and Honduras highlights patterns of unlawful practices by CBP officials 'designed to deny individuals their right under the law to apply for asylum'. Allegations include physical abuse, threats and intimidation, and reports of CBP officials falsely telling asylum-seekers that asylum is no longer available in the United States.[85] Reports of increased 'family separations' as a new policy to dissuade the illegal entry of immigrants and asylum-seekers additionally raise concerns about inhumane treatment and potential violations of children's rights.[86] This underscores the extent to which international order and domestic order are inherently linked, for 'world order is not merely about relations between sovereign states [but] it is also about order within states', including the fulfilment of social compacts and provision of basic rights and welfare.[87]

Conclusion

In affirming that 'an international order based on the rule of law … is essential for peaceful coexistence and cooperation among states',[88] member states at the World Summit acknowledged the importance of equally applied laws protecting fundamental rights for global stability. This article has explored challenges to the rule of law and international order posed by US violations of human rights principles in the realm of refugee protection. The right to asylum is clearly established in international customary law, and a strong case can be made that the principle of non-refoulement additionally rises to the status of *jus cogens*. The article also posited strong links between a responsibility to protect refugees fleeing genocide, war crimes, ethnic cleansing, and crimes against humanity and peremptory norms prohibiting such atrocities. If peremptory and customary legal norms are at work in non-refoulement and responsibilities to protect refugees fleeing *jus cogens* crimes, states are under a legal obligation not to contribute to the violation of these principles in any way. Moreover, the *jus cogens* nature of non-refoulement might oblige states to actively 'develop genuine responsibility sharing arrangements' given that the international refugee regime is dependent upon them.[89]

US actions contra the principle of non-refoulement and efforts to shirk refugee responsibility-sharing in the face of mass atrocity situations have significant consequences. These policies undermine legitimacy at both the domestic and the international level. Respect for human rights and non-discrimination are central to the democratic rule of law, which 'reinforces a political system's legitimacy by protecting the rights of citizens and foreigners'.[90] When domestic institutions do not follow and enforce human rights law, legitimacy is jeopardised and public trust is eroded. At the international level, the legitimate exercise of power relies in part on conformity with global human rights standards.[91] IR scholars might interpret intensified violations of these standards under the Trump administration as indicating a broader unravelling of the 'liberal leviathan' position, in which the United States works to support a liberal international order to 'dis-incentivize challengers to its position'.[92] As the United States retreats further from human rights commitments and respect for the rule of law, it erodes its legitimacy as 'a relatively predictable and cooperative hegemon'.[93]

US deviations from fundamental human rights principles also devalue international law as 'a predictor of state conduct and a means of holding states accountable'.[94] In addition to undermining its legitimacy as a democratic and hegemonic actor, US violations of international legal norms diminish its capacity to effectively apply external pressure to norm-violating states. Recent attempts to call attention to human rights violations in China and Cambodia, for example, were met with accusations of US hypocrisy and 'double standards' vis-à-vis its own human rights record.[95] This trend further weakens the collective power of the international community to induce human rights norm compliance. Such behaviour disrupts the broader architecture and foundations of global human rights governance. US violations of refugee protection norms, for instance, undermine the international refugee regime and the responsibility-sharing values on which it depends. Why should states with less material capability accept refugees fleeing mass atrocities or uphold the obligations of non-refoulement if the most powerful state in the international system does not adhere to these principles? Given its human rights and democracy promotion efforts abroad, US policies disregarding core refugee protection principles exacerbate perceptions of double standards and reinforce concerns that human rights instruments are merely instruments of neo-imperialism, or 'Western tool[s] that will never be used against Western powers'.[96] In this sense, US non-compliance with refugee protection principles tarnishes the human rights infrastructure writ large by highlighting grave problems of inequity in terms of enforcement. As notions of fairness, accountability and equally applied laws – all of which are fundamental to the international rule of law – are increasingly compromised, so too are the premises of a liberal international order.

Notes

1. For a summary of these perspectives see Constance Duncombe and Tim Dunne, 'After Liberal World Order', *International Affairs* 94, no. 1 (2018): 25–42.
2. G. John Ikenberry, 'The Future of Liberal World Order', *Japanese Journal of Political Science* 16, no. 3 (2015): 450–55, 450.
3. Seung-Whan Choi, 'Fighting Terrorism through the Rule of Law?', *Journal of Conflict Resolution* 54, no. 6 (2010): 940–66, 941.
4. Rosa Brooks, 'Drones and the International Rule of Law', *Ethics & International Affairs* 28, no. 1 (2014): 83–103.

5. UN Report of the Secretary-General, 'The Rule of Law and Transitional Justice in Conflict and Post-Conflict Societies' (23 August 2004) S/2004/616, 4, http://www.un.org/en/ga/search/view_doc.asp?symbol=S/2004/616 (accessed October 30, 2017).
6. Thomas Risse and Stephen C. Ropp, 'Introduction and Overview', Ch. 1 in *The Persistent Power of Human Rights: From Commitment to Compliance*, ed. Thomas Risse, Stephen C. Ropp, and Kathryn Sikkink (Cambridge and New York: Cambridge University Press, 2013), 3–25, 18.
7. '2005 World Summit Outcome', United Nations General Assembly A/RES/60/1 (24 October 2005), 27–29, https://www.un.org/ruleoflaw/files/2005%20World%20Summit%20Outcome.pdf (accessed January 7, 2018), para. 119.
8. See the working definition developed by the World Justice Project, https://worldjusticeproject.org/about-us/overview/what-rule-law (accessed 14 January 2018).
9. David P. Forsythe, *Human Rights in International Relations* (Cambridge and New York: Cambridge University Press, 2017), 18.
10. Michael J. Mazarr et al., *Measuring the Health of the Liberal International Order* (Santa Monica, CA: RAND Corporation, 2017), xii.
11. Ian Hurd, 'The International Rule of Law: Law and the Limit of Politics', *Ethics & International Affairs* 28, no. 1 (2014): 39–51, 43.
12. Susan D. Hyde, 'Catch Us If You Can: Election Monitoring and International Norm Diffusion', *American Journal of Political Science* 55, no. 2 (2011): 356–69.
13. Helen M. Kinsella, 'Discourses of Difference: Civilians, Combatants, and Compliance with the Laws of War', *Review of International Studies* 31 (2005): 163–85, 165.
14. Jay Winter, 'Veterans, Human Rights, and the Transformation of European Democracy', in *In War's Wake: International Conflict and the Fate of Liberal Democracy*, ed. Elizabeth Kier and Ronald R. Krebs (New York: Cambridge University Press, 2010), 121–38, 124.
15. Judith Kelley, 'Who Keeps International Commitments and Why? The International Criminal Court and Bilateral Nonsurrender Agreements', *The American Political Science Review* 101, no. 3 (2007): 573–89, 586.
16. Larry May, *Global Justice and Due Process* (Cambridge and New York: Cambridge University Press, 2011), 120–21.
17. William E. Conklin, 'The Peremptory Norms of the International Community', *European Journal of International Law* 23, no. 3 (2012): 837–61, 847.
18. David Armstrong, Theo Farrell and Helene Lambert, *International Law and International Relations* (Cambridge: Cambridge University Press, 2012), 214.
19. Peter Sutch, 'Normative IR Theory and the Legalization of International Politics: The Dictates of Humanity and of the Public Conscience as a Vehicle for Global Justice', *Journal of International Political Theory* 8, no. 1–2 (2012): 1–24, 14.
20. Colin Harvey, 'Time for Reform? Refugees, Asylum-Seekers, and Protection Under International Human Rights Law', *Refugee Survey Quarterly* 34, no. 1 (2015): 43–60, 46.
21. Office of the United Nations High Commissioner on Refugees, *Refugee Protection in International Law: UNHCR's Global Consultations International Protection* (Cambridge: Cambridge University Press, 2003), 150.
22. See Chantal Marie-Jeanne Bostock, 'The International Legal Obligations Owed to the Asylum Seekers on the *MV Tampa*', *International Journal of Refugee Law* 14, no. 2/3 (2002): 279–301; and Alice Edwards, 'Temporary Protection, Derogation and the 1951 Refugee Convention', *Melbourne Journal of International Law* 13, no. 2 (2012): 595–635.
23. See, for example, Jean Allain, 'The *Jus Cogens* Nature of *Non-Refoulement*', *International Journal of Refugee Law* 13, no. 4 (2002): 533–58; Erika de Wet, 'The Prohibition of Torture as an International Norm of *Jus Cogens* and Its Implications for National and Customary Law', *European Journal of International Law* 15, no. 1 (2004): 97–121; and Sigit Riyanto, 'The Refoulement Principle and Its Relevance in the International Law System', *Indonesia Journal of International Law* 7, no. 4 (2010): 695–715.
24. Allain, '*Jus Cogens* Nature of *Non-Refoulement*', 539.

25. 'Cartagena Declaration on Refugees, Colloquium on the International Protection of Refugees in Central America, Mexico and Panama' (November 1984), Section III, https://www.oas.org/dil/1984_cartagena_declaration_on_refugees.pdf (accessed 29 October 2017); and 'Brazil Declaration: A Framework for Cooperation and Regional Solidarity to Strengthen the International Protection of Refugees, Displaced and Stateless Persons in Latin America and the Caribbean' (3 December 2014), 2, http://www.acnur.org/t3/fileadmin/Documentos/BDL/2014/9865.pdf (accessed 29 October 2017).
26. UNHCR, *Refugee Protection in International Law*, 155.
27. Rene Bruin and Kees Wouters, 'Terrorism and the Non-Derogability of *Non-Refoulement*', *International Journal of Refugee Law* 15, no. 1 (2003): 5–29, 25.
28. Sylvie Da Lomba, *The Right to Seek Refugee Status in the European Union* (Oxford: Intersentia, 2004), 7.
29. UNHCR, *Refugee Protection in International Law*, 150.
30. Aoife Duffy, 'Expulsion to Face Torture? *Non-Refoulement* in International Law', *International Journal of Refugee Law* 20, no. 3 (2008): 373–90, 390.
31. See Alice Farmer, 'Non-Refoulement and Jus Cogens: Limiting Anti-Terror Measures that Threaten Refugee Protection', *Georgetown Immigration Law Journal* 23, no. 1 (2008): 1–38; and Shirley Llain Arenilla, 'Violations to the Principle of Non-Refoulement Under the Asylum Policy of the United States', *Anuario Mexicano de Derecho Internacional* XV (2015): 283–322, 288.
32. Guy S. Goodwin-Gill, 'The Right to Seek Asylum: Interception at Sea and the Principle of *Non-Refoulement*', *International Journal of Refugee Law* 23, no. 3 (2011): 443–57, 445.
33. '2005 World Summit Outcome', para. 139.
34. 'Resolution 2150', *UN Security Council* (16 April 2014) S/Res/2150, http://www.globalr2p.org/media/files/resolution-2150.pdf (accessed 7 January 2018).
35. Jennifer M. Welsh, 'Norm Contestation and the Responsibility to Protect', *Global Responsibility to Protect* 5 (2013): 365–96, 366.
36. See Brian Barbour and Brian Gorlick, 'Embracing the "Responsibility to Protect": A Repertoire of Measures Including Asylum for Potential Victims', *International Journal of Refugee Law* 20, no. 4 (2008): 533–66; Alise Coen, 'R2P, Global Governance, and the Syrian Refugee Crisis', *International Journal of Human Rights* 19, no. 8 (2015): 1044–58; Chloë Gilgan, 'Exploring the Link between R2P and Refugee Protection: Arriving at Resettlement', *Global Responsibility to Protect* 9, no. 4 (2017): 366–94; and Jason Ralph and James Souter, 'A Special Responsibility to Protect: the UK, Australia and the Rise of Islamic State', *International Affairs* 91, no. 4 (2015): 709–23.
37. Barbour and Gorlick, 'Embracing the "Responsibility to Protect"', 541; and Sonja Grover, 'R2P and the Syrian Crisis: When Semantics Becomes a Matter of Life or Death', *The International Journal of Human Rights* 19, no. 8 (2015): 1112–28, 1125.
38. Luke Glanville, 'The Responsibility to Protect Beyond Borders', *Human Rights Law Review* 12, no. 1 (2012): 1–32, 27.
39. Benjamin A. Valentino, 'The True Costs of Humanitarian Intervention: The Hard Truth About a Noble Notion', *Foreign Affairs* 90, no. 6 (2011): 60–73.
40. See Luara Ferracioli, 'The Appeal and Danger of a New Refugee Convention', *Social Theory and Practice* 40, no. 1 (2014): 123–44; and Matthew J. Gibney, 'Refugees and Justice between States', *European Journal of Political Theory* 14, no. 4 (2015): 448–63.
41. Gabriela Baczynska, 'EU Proposes Scheme to Share Out Asylum Seekers', *Reuters* (4 May 2016), https://www.reuters.com/article/us-europe-migrants-eu-asylum/eu-proposes-scheme-to-share-out-asylum-seekers-idUSKCN0XV13G (accessed 7 January 2018).
42. See Michael Barutciski and Astri Suhrke, 'Lessons from the Kosovo Refugee Crisis: Innovations in Protection and Burden-Sharing', *Journal of Refugee Studies* 14, no. 2 (2001): 95–134; James Souter, 'Towards a Theory of Asylum as Reparation for Past Injustice', *Political Studies* 62, no. 2 (2014): 326–42; Ralph and Souter, 'A Special Responsibility to Protect'; and Alise Coen, 'Capable and Culpable? The United States, RtoP, and Refugee Responsibility-Sharing', *Ethics and International Affairs* 31, no. 1 (2017): 71–92

43. Ikenberry, 'Future of Liberal World Order', 451.
44. Nicolas Guilhot, *Democracy Makers: Human Rights and International Order* (New York: Columbia University Press, 2005), 19.
45. Kathryn Sikkink, 'The United States and Torture: Does the Spiral Model Work?' Ch. 8 in *The Persistent Power of Human Rights: From Commitment to Compliance*, ed. Thomas Risse, Stephen C. Ropp, and Kathryn Sikkink (Cambridge and New York: Cambridge University Press, 2013), 145.
46. Chris Nwachukwu Okeke and James A. R. Nafziger, 'United States Migration Law: Essentials for Comparison', *The American Journal of Comparative Law* 54 (2006): 531–52, 532.
47. Joan Fitzpatrick, 'The International Dimension of US Refugee Law', *Berkeley Journal of International Law* 15, no. 1 (1997): 1–26, 25.
48. Thomas Gammeltoft-Hansen, 'International Refugee Law and Refugee Policy: The Case of Deterrence Policies', *Journal of Refugee Studies* 27, no. 4 (2014): 1–22, 4.
49. 'Legal Obligations of the United States Under Article 33 of the Refugee Convention', *The United States Department of Justice* (12 December 1991), https://www.justice.gov/file/23326/download (accessed 1 November 2017), 87.
50. Paula Ioanide, *The Emotional Politics of Racism: How Feelings Trump Facts in an era of Colorblindness* (Stanford, CA: Stanford University Press, 2015), 133.
51. J. Anna Cabot, 'Problems Faced by Mexican Asylum Seekers in the United States', *Journal on Migration and Human Security* 2, no. 4 (2014): 361–77, 363.
52. 'Beyond Detention: A Global Strategy to Support Governments to End the Detention of Asylum-Seekers and Refugees, Progress Report', UNHCR (18 August 2016), 82, http://www.unhcr.org/en-us/protection/detention/57b579e47/unhcr-global-strategy-beyond-detention-progress-report.html (accessed 22 November 2017).
53. Alice Edwards, 'The Optional Protocol to the Convention against Torture and the Detention of Refugees', *The International and Comparative Law Quarterly* 57, no. 4 (2008): 789–825, 790.
54. Cathryn Costello, 'Human Rights and the Elusive Universal Subject: Immigration Detention Under International Human Rights and EU Law', *Indiana Journal of Global Legal Studies* 19, no. 1 (2012): 257–303, 276.
55. James C. Hathaway, 'Refugees and Asylum', in *Foundations of International Migration Law*, ed. B. Opeskin et al. (Cambridge: Cambridge University Press, 2012), 183.
56. Celia Medrano, 'Securing Protection for De Facto Refugees: The Case of Central America's Northern Triangle', *Ethics & International Affairs* 31, no. 2 (2017): 129–42, 129.
57. Ediberto Román, *Those Damned Immigrants: America's Hysteria over Undocumented Immigration* (New York and London: New York University Press, 2013), 33.
58. David R. Roediger, *Working Toward Whiteness: How America's Immigrants Became White* (New York: Basic Books, 2005), 207.
59. Simon Chesterman, 'An International Rule of Law?' *The American Journal of Comparative Law* 56, no. 2 (2008): 331–62, 342.
60. Guillermo A. O'Donnell, 'Why the Rule of Law Matters', *Journal of Democracy* 15, no. 4 (2004): 32–46, 45.
61. Fiona de Londras, 'Can Counter-Terrorist Internment Ever be Legitimate?', *Human Rights Quarterly* 33, no. 3 (2011): 593–619, 607.
62. Andy J. Rottman, 'The Path to Asylum in the US and the Determinants for Who Gets in and Why', *The International Migration Review* 43, no. 1 (2009): 3–34, 29.
63. 'Operation Liberty Shield', FEMA (17 March 2003), https://www.fema.gov/news-release/2003/03/17/operation-liberty-shield (accessed 14 January 2018).
64. Michael Welch and Liza Schuster, 'Detention of Asylum Seekers in the US, UK, France, and Germany: A Critical View of the Globalizing Culture of Control', *Criminal Justice* 5, no. 4 (2005): 331–55, 336.
65. Arenilla, 'Violations to the Principle of Non-Refoulement', 300–01.
66. Hathaway, 'Refugees and Asylum', 190.
67. 'Executive Order Protecting the Nation from Foreign Terrorist Entry into the United States', *The White House* (27 January 2017), https://www.whitehouse.gov/presidential-actions/

executive-order-protecting-nation-foreign-terrorist-entry-united-states/ (accessed 4 November 2017). Note that the order was revised several times over the course of 2017 amid evolving legal challenges and court interpretations.

68. Goodwin-Gill, 'Right to Seek Asylum', 445.
69. Meg Satterthwaite and Alexander Zetes, 'Explainer on the Legal Obligation Not to Return Refugees and How Trump's Exec Order Breaks It', *Just Security* (4 February 2017), https://www.justsecurity.org/37305/explainer-legal-obligation-return-refugees-trumps-executive-order-breaks/ (accessed 4 November 2017).
70. Rottman, 'Path to Asylum in the US', 7.
71. See Nick Cumming-Bruce, 'ISIS Committed Genocide against Yazidis in Syria and Iraq, UN Panel Says', *New York Times* (16 June 2016), https://www.nytimes.com/2016/06/17/world/middleeast/isis-genocide-yazidi-un.html (accessed 14 January 2018); and 'These Are the Crimes We Are Fleeing', *Human Rights Watch* (3 October 2017), https://www.hrw.org/report/2017/10/03/these-are-crimes-we-are-fleeing/justice-syria-swedish-and-german-courts (accessed 14 January 2018).
72. Alex J. Bellamy and Ruben Reike, 'The Responsibility to Protect and International Law', *Global Responsibility to Protect* 2, no. 3 (2010): 267–86, 276.
73. Chandra Lekha Sriram, *Globalizing Justice for Mass Atrocities: A Revolution in Accountability* (London and New York: Routledge, 2005), 43.
74. James C. Hathaway, 'Executive (Dis)order and Refugees – the Trump Policy's Blindness to International Law', *Just Security* (1 February 2017), https://www.justsecurity.org/37113/executive-disorder-refugees-the-trump-policys-blindness-international-law/ (accessed 4 November 2017).
75. 'Presidential Proclamation Enhancing Vetting Capabilities and Processes for Detecting Attempted Entry into the United States by Terrorists or Other Public-Safety Threats', The White House Office of the Press Secretary (24 September 2017), https://www.whitehouse.gov/the-press-office/2017/09/24/enhancing-vetting-capabilities-and-processes-detecting-attempted-entry (accessed 11 November 2017).
76. Jay Shooster, 'Trump's Immigration Policy Risks Violating International Law – Alienates US Allies', *Just Security* (27 January 2017), https://www.justsecurity.org/36834/trumps-immigration-restrictions-risk-violating-international-law-cutting-foreign-allies-support/ (accessed 11 November 2017).
77. Cathryn Costello and Michelle Foster, 'Non-Refoulement as Custom and *Jus Cogens*? Putting the Prohibition to the Test', in *Netherlands Yearbook of International Law 2015: Jus Cogens: Quo Vadis*? ed. Maarten den Heijer and Harmen van der Wilt (The Hague, Netherlands: Springer, 2016) 273–328, 315–16.
78. 'Historical Arrivals Broken Down by Region (1975–Present)', US Department of State Refugee Processing Center (5 October 2017), http://www.wrapsnet.org/admissions-and-arrivals/ (accessed 19 November 2017).
79. 'Refugee Admissions Report: October 31, 2017', US Department of State Refugee Processing Center (31 October 2017), http://www.wrapsnet.org/admissions-and-arrivals/ (accessed 19 November 2017).
80. Colum Lynch, 'Trump to Cut Number of Refugees in US by More than Half', *Foreign Policy* (26 September 2017), http://foreignpolicy.com/2017/09/26/trump-to-cut-number-of-refugees-in-u-s-by-more-than-half/ (accessed 19 November 2017).
81. For a discussion of US culpability-based responsibilities to protect Syrian refugees, see Coen, 'Capable and Culpable'.
82. Krishnadev Calamur, 'Trump's New Refugee Policy Targets These 11 Countries', *The Atlantic* (25 October 2017), https://www.theatlantic.com/international/archive/2017/10/us-refugees-11-countries/543933/ (accessed 19 November 2017).
83. Yeganeh Torbati, 'Under Trump Plan, Refugees from 11 Countries Face Additional US Barriers', *Reuters* (24 October 2017), https://www.reuters.com/article/us-usa-immigration-refugees/under-trump-plan-refugees-from-11-countries-face-additional-u-s-barriers-idUSKBN1CT2IV (accessed 19 November 2017).

84. See, for example, Carlo Allegri, 'Trump Plans New Guidelines to Speed Deportation of Asylum-Seekers: Draft Memo', *Reuters* (19 February 2017), http://www.newsweek.com/trump-guidelines-speed-deportations-asylum-seekers-558520 (accessed 14 January 2018); and Conchita Cruz and Swapna Reddy, 'Why Deportation Could Mean Death for Some Refugees', *Time* (9 March 2017), http://time.com/4696017/deportation-death-refugees-asylum/ (accessed 14 January 2018).
85. Ryan Devereaux, 'US Illegally Denying Immigrants their Right to Seek Asylum at the Mexican Border, According to Lawsuit', *The Intercept* (16 November 2017), https://theintercept.com/2017/11/16/immigration-asylum-seekers-denied-border-entry-lawsuit/ (accessed 14 January 2018).
86. Clark Mindock, 'Trump Administration Considering Family Separation Policy for Asylum Seekers', *The Independent* (22 December 2017), http://www.independent.co.uk/news/world/americas/us-politics/trump-family-separation-policy-asylum-seekers-deportation-ice-a8125546.html (accessed 14 January 2018).
87. George Sørensen, *Rethinking the New World Order* (London and New York: Palgrave Macmillan, 2016), 31.
88. '2005 World Summit Outcome', para. 134.
89. Costello and Foster, 'Non-Refoulement as Custom and *Jus Cogens*', 317.
90. Choi, 'Fighting Terrorism through the Rule of Law', 948.
91. Forsythe, *Human Rights in International Relations*, 10.
92. Nikolas Gvosdev, 'State of the Union: The Era of the Liberal Leviathan is Over', *Ethics & International Affairs* (31 January 2018), https://www.ethicsandinternationalaffairs.org/2018/state-union-era-liberal-leviathan/ (accessed 31 January 2018).
93. G. John Ikenberry, *Liberal Order & Imperial Ambition* (Cambridge: Polity Press, 2006), 190.
94. Brooks, 'Drones and the International Rule of Law', 98.
95. 'China Swipes Back at US in Annual Rights Report', *Reuters* (28 February 2014), https://www.reuters.com/article/us-china-usa-rights/china-swipes-back-at-u-s-in-annual-rights-report-idUSBREA1R0C220140228 (accessed 27 October 2017); and 'Cambodia's Hun Sen Renews Criticism of United States Amid Escalating Row', *Reuters* (11 October 2017), https://www.reuters.com/article/us-cambodia-politics/cambodias-hun-sen-renews-criticism-of-united-states-amid-escalating-row-idUSKBN1CG0RX (accessed 27 October 2017).
96. David Armstrong, 'Evolving Conceptions of Justice in International Law', *Review of International Studies* 37, no. 5 (2011): 2121–36, 2133.

Disclosure statement

No potential conflict of interest was reported by the authors.

ORCID

Alise Coen http://orcid.org/0000-0002-5239-3358

The harbinger theory of terrorism and the rule of law: the danger of 'balancing' non-derogable rights against security when relying on threat assessments produced by self-interested intelligence agencies

Ryan Alford

ABSTRACT

The harbinger theory of terrorism holds that the events of 9/11 presaged an inevitable set of mass terror attacks that would constitute an existential threat to the Global North. It has become the key premise of the argument that in an era purportedly defined by the threat of transnational terrorism, these nations must reject all limits on the measures they take to reinforce state security. This theory is incompatible on its face with non-derogable rights, which are essential to any instantiation of the rule of law in any international or domestic constitutional order. This article demonstrates that accepting this theory inevitably leads to the erosion of these rights, to the point that in a future public order emergency (which the harbinger theory holds to be inevitable), the rule of law will be abrogated. This is true even in nations where there have been no substantial terrorist attacks. Developments in Canada demonstrate that when the harbinger theory and the premise that rights must be balanced against security are accepted, this erosion accelerates.

1. Introduction

The rule of law is not merely a regulative ideal. It is instantiated into the legal framework of every nation that has created a form of government defined by a constitution, whether written or unwritten. Its primary purpose is to limit the powers of those governments, preserving a political order in which authority can only be considered lawful when it exists within constitutional bounds; the outermost of those limits is the set of rights commonly recognised by humanity. Conversely, a purely formal conception of the rule of law, in which the absolute limits of governmental power are arbitrary and infinitely malleable, has never existed.

As a historical matter, every existing constitutional order was catalysed by the recognition that certain rights must be given special protection, such that they might never be violated even when reasons of state are invoked. Those rights, which were in dispute over centuries of struggle to limit the special prerogatives of government, attained a special status in both constitutional and international law. Accordingly, these rights –

which binding international conventions insist can never be violated, even during the most serious public emergencies – are universally recognised peremptory norms. Three key examples are the right not to be extrajudicially killed, not to be tortured, and not to be subjected to indefinite or prolonged arbitrary detention, all of which are now under serious pressure in more states than ever before in the twenty-first century.

The special relationship between these rights and the rule of law has two dimensions. First, the refusal of states to abandon doctrines, such as reasons of state, as a basis for violating these rights during self-declared emergencies was the primary impetus for the development of constitutionalism and the rule of law. Second, because the peremptory norms constitute a commonly recognised outer limit of governmental power that applies under all circumstances, systemic violations of these rights within a nation provide an indisputable basis for a conclusion that it is no longer a rule-of-law state.

The possibility that one might be forced to conclude that a nation which is nominally a constitutional democracy is, in fact, no longer a rule-of-law state (owing to doctrines that allow the government to violate peremptory norms with impunity) is no longer hypothetical. The United States has an ever-expanding targeted killing programme which its Attorney General acknowledged could, in his view, be used against American citizens within its own borders;[1] its interrogation manuals contain special annexes that describe techniques that amount to cruel and inhuman treatment,[2] and its laws continue to contemplate indefinite arbitrary detention at the pleasure of the executive.

This article will demonstrate that the trajectory of the constitutional order of the United States beyond the outer limits of the rule of law is not unique, even if most other nations in the Global North have not progressed as far in that direction to date. The second section will detail the forces that propel states back towards the adoption of exceptional doctrines in the era of transnational terrorism, focusing in particular on the function of the harbinger theory. The third section will demonstrate how the unquestioned adoption of this theory has driven governments to adopt legislation that places non-derogable rights under intense pressure, even where there have been no significant terrorist attacks. The fourth section will detail how the new framework of 'balancing' rights against security entails a repudiation of the concept of non-derogability in practice, particularly when all the information on the appropriateness of the balancing point relies on the assessments of intelligence agencies with a clear self-interest in exaggerating the threat and which consistently promote the harbinger theory.

With these agencies' thumbs on the scale, the balance will always tilt away from rights and towards security. In practice, this gives governments a free hand to violate non-derogable rights; when a major public order emergency finally arrives in states where these rights have been eroded away, the rule of law will not survive intact. Accordingly, critical scholarship should address the role of intelligence agencies and the dynamics that empower them in the degeneration of the rule of law, rather than focusing exclusively on the formal or theoretical elements of the shortcomings of existing legal regimes.

2. The war on terror as a rupture of norms and paradigms

Before the Second World War, certain international bodies suggested that state sovereignty was not an absolute bar to finding a nation responsible for failing to observe the obligations of international law.[3] However, the international order – in the form of the

League of Nations – was incapable of holding states that committed even the most egregious violations responsible, as was the case after the Italian invasion of Ethiopia, in which the Italian Army used poison gas extensively and fired on the facilities of the Red Cross.[4]

The horrors of the Second World War served as the stimulus for a new and more durable international order, in which reasons of state could no longer be used to justify violations of human rights or the crime of aggression. This new paradigm was framed by the erection of the United Nations (UN) and the adoption of the International Covenant on Civil and Political Rights; it was cemented and reinforced by the memory of the war crimes tribunals conducted by the occupying powers in Germany and Japan.

In this new regime of international human rights and international humanitarian law, the refusal of a state to recognise these limitations on its political authority is formally irrelevant, as this set of peremptory norms was recognised by the international community as binding at all times. These create rights from which no derogation is permitted.[5] However, in the aftermath of the 9/11 attacks, these obligations to observe certain rights as absolute were to be tested by new theories of national security, which held that this paradigm of peremptory norms was obsolete; as will be detailed in this section, the structural tension between these arguments and the concept of the peremptory norms is substantial, and has periodically led to rifts in the constitutional order of numerous states in the Global North, shearing them away from the foundations of the twentieth century's international order.

2.1. The ICCPR versus the harbinger theory of international terrorism

The two foundational documents of the new international order of human rights are the Universal Declaration of Human Rights and the International Covenant on Civil and Political Rights (ICCPR), which was proposed in the immediate aftermath of the Second World War; the Covenant responded to the UN's founding conference's directive to create a 'Declaration on the Essential Rights of Man'.

Articles 6–27 of the ICCPR list these rights; Article 4 establishes a regime for their derogation, by providing that during a 'public emergency which threatens the life of the nation' states 'may take measures derogating from the obligations to observe those rights'. However, a subset of these rights cannot be infringed even during an emergency of that magnitude: these comprise the set of non-derogable rights.

2.1.1. Non-derogable rights: a bulwark against the sovereign

The conditions for and the limits on states' ability to derogate was clarified by the Siracusa Principles on the Limitation and Derogation Principles in the ICCPR,[6] which was adopted by the UN Commission on Human Rights in 1984.[7] These principles affirm the ICCPR's absolute ban on torture and extrajudicial killing, and clarify the prohibition on indefinite arbitrary detention. They further state that an emergency can only justify derogation if it

> affects the whole of the population and either the whole or part of the territory of the State, and … threatens the physical integrity of the population, the political independence or the territorial integrity of the State or the existence or basic functioning of institutions indispensable to ensure and protect the rights recognized in the Covenant.[8]

The affirmation that non-derogable rights cannot be infringed even if the state is in fact being destroyed was not done thoughtlessly: it stems directly from the international community's rejection of the invocation of the safety of the state during internal emergencies as a justification for the violation of human rights, as the Nuremberg Tribunals had refused to exonerate those guilty of war crimes allegedly committed to preserve the existence of Germany when it was engaged in a state of total war.[9]

2.1.2. The harbinger theory: terrorism presented as existential threat

The attacks of 11 September 2001 killed 3000 people and caused 10 billion dollars' worth of damage. This scale of casualties and destruction was not unprecedented, even if the wars of the twentieth century are excluded: the Bhopal chemical disaster caused more deaths; hurricanes routinely cause property damage at a rate 10 times higher. The 9/11 attacks assumed an outsized significance for two reasons: because they connect to a profound fear of terrorism, and because they were accepted as proof that they prefigured more serious – or even existential – threats to the state, which were allegedly in the hands of a uniquely dangerous enemy: the terrorist.

Terrorism has no special status in international law. The United Nations General Assembly has failed to agree to a Comprehensive Convention on International Terrorism despite engaging in negotiations that began in 2002. However, despite lacking any legal definition, the word 'terrorism' possesses clear political force: 'the peculiar semantic power of the term, beyond its literal signification, is its capacity to stigmatize, delegitimize, denigrate, and dehumanize those at whom it is directed, including political opponents'.[10]

The common definition of terrorism is circular, as it is used as a label for attacks that are committed by 'terrorists' against 'innocent' targets. These labels are assigned on a transparently political basis:

> Left to its political meaning, terrorism easily falls prey to change that suits the interests of particular states at particular times. The Taliban and Osama bin Laden were once called freedom fighters (mujahideen) and backed by the CIA when they were resisting the Soviet occupation of Afghanistan. Now they are at the top of the international terror lists.[11]

While the 9/11 attacks would qualify as terrorism under any possible definition of that term (as they were an unprovoked attack against a civilian population), the fact that certain incidents appear to unambiguously fall within it masks a tension at the semantic core of the concept related to the identity of its perpetrators, which is closely connected to its historical genesis.

Analysis of the modern concept of terrorism owes much to its use as a tool in American foreign policy during the 1980s: 'The rise of the scholarly effort began soon as the Reagan administration declared "terrorism" as one of its greatest enemies',[12] a declaration that came in the wake of the Beirut barracks bombing of 23 October 1983, an attack by the Lebanese Islamic Jihad that precipitated a humiliating withdrawal of American forces. Conversely, Reagan was quick to excuse the irregular military forces he supported in low-intensity conflicts against his adversaries in Afghanistan and Nicaragua: the Contras, despite being implicated in numerous atrocities, were given the status of being 'the moral equivalent of our founding fathers'.[13] By using this political lens, the United States could justify actions contrary to general principles of international humanitarian law in support of the Contras, such as producing and disseminating a manual that advised them how to rationalise the killing of civilians.[14] The Contras, it should be noted, were a non-state armed force frequently implicated in attacks on non-combatants:

'No one doubts that the contras have committed serious abuses. A report last year by the respected human rights group Americas Watch found that they have carried out widespread executions, torture and kidnappings of government sympathizers'.[15]

The distinction drawn by the Reagan administration between the freedom fighter and the terrorist hinges on the characterisation of the actions and motivations of those who engage in attacks on civilians – namely, whether they are to be feared. Terrorists – a label that no one adopts – are characterised by their purported willingness to use political violence not to achieve rational goals, but rather because of an inchoate desire to destroy: President Bush argued that the 9/11 attackers 'hate our freedoms … these terrorists kill not merely to end lives, but to disrupt and end a way of life'.[16]

The vacuity of this politically convenient definition is best demonstrated by the fact that in the first two years after Osama Bin Laden founded al-Qaeda, he was working closely with Gulbiddin Hekmatyar, who received by conservative estimates approximately $600,000,000 of American aid. In 1988 and 1989 they fought the Soviets occupying Afghanistan exclusively (frequently without distinguishing between Soviet armed forces and civilian support personnel and Afghan civilian 'collaborators'), with weapons provided by the United States.[17] Despite the fact that al-Qaeda needed no weapons larger than box cutters to perpetrate the 9/11 attacks, it quickly became an article of faith in Western intelligence services that attacks that would threaten the existence of these states were being planned and would soon be executed by pitiless terrorists.

Robert Diab has labelled this new dogma 'the harbinger theory' and described its function as follows:

> 9/11 was the harbinger of a new order of terror, in which further attacks in North America are likely to occur at some point in the near future, on a similar or greater scale as 9/11, possibly, but not necessarily, involving weapons of mass destruction … [a]nd on this basis, earlier assumptions about the absolute limits of state force against individuals have come to seem untenable or imprudent.[18]

Diab's conclusion is that intelligence reports of plans or 'chatter' by terrorists to engage in attacks using biological weapons or 'dirty bombs' are not plausible given the technical limitations and logistical complications of this endeavour. However, in no small part due to the general acceptance of the harbinger theory and public clamour to be protected from further terrorist attacks, in the 16 years of the 'war on terror' that followed 9/11 the constitutional order of the United States devolved to the point that it can no longer be considered a fully functional rule-of-law state, primarily because its executive can now violate non-derogable rights with impunity.[19] By the beginning of the Trump administration, 'there are no longer any non-derogable rights. Put otherwise, all constitutional and human rights have proven to be derogable, including rights against torture, cruelty, and "extra-judicial" killing'.[20] In particular, Diab and others refer to the targeted killing programme and the use of torture at the Guantanamo Bay Detention Camp.

The implosion of the rule of law in the United States occurred despite the absence of the predicted terror attacks on a scale larger than or even equivalent to 9/11 – the deadliest attack since then within the United States was the Orlando nightclub shooting of 2016, in which 49 were killed: before that, the deadliest act of terrorism during that decade was the Fort Hood shooting of 2009, in which 13 were killed. (This range of casualties is comparable in scale to the most recent and apolitical mass shootings in the United

States: 58 were killed in the 2017 Las Vegas attack and 17 at the Parkland shootings in 2018). There is no evidence, or even claim from its intelligence agencies, to have thwarted attacks on the same scale as 9/11, at least after the fanciful allegations that José Padilla was involved in a plot to detonate a so-called 'dirty bomb' were withdrawn.[21]

That said, one might argue that the degeneration of the rule of law in the United States occurred under conditions that are *sui generis*, owing to a terrorist attack of a magnitude not seen previously or since, and the existence of a peculiar and politicised anxiety about terrorism in that country. Accordingly one might conclude that there is no general threat to the rule of law internationally, or at least not one connected to the pressures of transnational terrorism and the possibility of disproportionate responses that endanger non-derogable rights. However, the next section will provide a representative counterexample by demonstrating that similar dynamics are at play in another nation despite the absence of any significant terror attacks in the twenty-first century, and where a fear of terrorism was not promoted as a justification for aggressive foreign policy in the twentieth. That nation is Canada.

3. Canada: steady erosion of rights despite the absence of terrorism

The mounting pressures on non-derogable rights created by the adoption of the harbinger theory of terrorism have proven to be incessant, even in countries (unlike Spain and France) that have experienced no large-scale terrorist violence in this new era of transnational terrorism allegedly inaugurated by the 9/11 attacks. Canada is a pertinent example of how this pressure can create fissures in the constitutional order, which might lead to a total rupture of its rule of law in a future public order emergency. There are two sets of legislative changes that prefigure challenges to the inviolability of non-derogable rights in Canada, each of which came in the wake of what appear to be in retrospect minor terrorist attacks; their significance was magnified and distorted when viewed through the lens of the harbinger theory.

3.1. The aftermath of 9/11 in Canada: the Anti-terrorism Act, 2001

The Parliament of Canada rushed to pass national security legislation in the wake of the 9/11 attacks; Bill C-41 was fast-tracked, received Royal Assent on 18 December and was enacted as the Anti-terrorism Act, 2001. The Act has two particularly troublesome provisions. The first was the introduction of a durable regime of preventative detention into Canadian law.[22] The second was a set of modifications to the rules governing the detention of non-citizens suspected to be a threat to the security of Canada.[23] This new detention regime allows for the indefinite detention without bail of any permanent resident or foreign national, on the basis of a security certificate issued by two cabinet ministers.

These provisions authorising preventative and, for non-citizens, indefinite detention rely 'heavily on the word of the Canadian Security Intelligence Service (CSIS)'.[24] CSIS need only allege that the suspect is a 'member of an organization that there are reasonable grounds to believe engages in, or will engage in … terrorism'.[25] In the United Kingdom, virtually identical provisions for indefinite detention came under vigorous judicial criticism: Lord Nicholls of Birkenhead declared them to be 'anathema in any country that observes the rule of law'.[26] This is due to the fact that, as Colleen Bell notes:

> [P]reventative, indefinite detention, without charges, conviction, or the minimum standards of criminal jurisprudence is no less than an exercise of sovereign will. It produces the provisions for detainment of those only deemed to constitute a threat, allowing the state to extend its own domain of jurisdiction for action. This codifies such sovereign acts within the realm of law, while simultaneously evading the rule of law.[27]

This is also directly contrary to the provisions of the Siracusa Principles, which establish that the right not to be subjected to indefinite arbitrary detention is non-derogable. Additionally, many of those detained by means of security certificates were held pending deportation to countries in which they would likely be tortured: this would constitute refoulement in violation of Canada's obligations under the Convention Against Torture.[28] That said, to date the Canadian judiciary has restrained the government from violating these non-derogable rights in important ways: the Supreme Court of Canada has insisted procedures be created that allow for the scrutiny of CSIS's allegations in detention hearings (which has led to embarrassing dressing-downs from the courts about the paucity and poor quality of its intelligence reports)[29] and, owing to judicial review of deportation orders, it appears Canada has yet to deport anyone from Canada to a country where they have been tortured.[30] However, the Arar Inquiry did reveal that Canadian intelligence officials facilitated the refoulement of a Canadian citizen to Syria, where he was tortured.[31] Additionally, it is notable that non-derogable rights came under severe pressure in Canada owing to legislation prompted by a terror attack in another country. A substantially more problematic bill would become law after the first high-profile terror attacks in Canada since 2001, in which only two people were killed.

3.2. The 2014 terror attacks and Bill C-51: rights in the balance

Two terror attacks occurred in Canada in rapid succession. On 20 October 2014, Martin Rouleau intentionally rammed his car into another vehicle occupied by two members of the Canadian Armed Forces in the parking lot of a suburban shopping centre, killing one. The perpetrator, who had converted to Islam a year before the attack, reportedly claimed to have done so for religious reasons in a subsequent call to a 911 operator,[32] while his relatives claimed that 'he needed psychiatric help'.[33] On 22 October, Michael Zehaf-Bibeau, armed with a vintage lever-action hunting rifle, shot a member of the ceremonial guard at the Canadian National War Memorial and exchanged fire with the security officers inside the Centre Block of the Parliament of Canada. This second attacker was a homeless man with a long history of drug addiction and petty crime who was thought by his friends to be mentally ill after he claimed 'the devil is after him'.[34]

The Government of Canada was quick to label these attacks as 'ISIL-inspired terrorism' (Islamic State of Iraq and the Levant) despite the fact that the connection between the perpetrators and transnational terrorist groups was notional, or at most a matter of self-aggrandising and purely subjective affiliation by two deeply disturbed individuals. While a poll released one month later revealed that a plurality of Canadians attributed the attacks to mental illness,[35] the government wasted 'no time in seizing on the incident to promote its fear-mongering agenda over terrorism, which includes pending legislation to vest its intelligence agency, CSIS, with more spying and secrecy powers in the name of fighting Islamic State in Iraq and Syria'.[36] These measures (detailed below) include the assertion of a power to disrupt terror plots using means that would violate the Charter. As noted above, Diab has concluded that there is no existential threat from terrorism, and even if there were, certain rights protected by the rule of law remain non-derogable.

Bill C-51, enacted as the Anti-terrorism Act, 2015, was introduced in Parliament two months after these attacks. The Act was:

> [T]he most controversial piece of legislation of the new century. In addition to prompting widespread protests, it was the subject of an open letter signed by over one hundred law professors and a joint statement by five former Supreme Court justices, seven former solicitors general and ministers of justice ... each of whom called for substantial amendments or the bill's withdrawal.[37]

The most controversial provisions of Bill C-51 allow CSIS to request special warrants from a Justice of the Federal Court (in a closed and confidential proceeding) that would authorise CSIS to do what, in the government's view, would otherwise violate the Canadian Charter of Rights and Freedoms. As the non-derogable rights protected by Article 4 are instantiated into Canadian law via the Charter, these authorisation provisions indicated that the government believed that these warrants would supersede or bypass the protections of Canada's domestic and international obligations. Unlike the Emergencies Act, 1988, the Anti-terrorism Act, 2015, makes no mention of Canada's obligation to treat certain rights as non-derogable.[38]

Detention warrants were explicitly contemplated by the legislators who debated Bill C-51; as the new warrants could request the authorisation of infringing more than one right, CSIS could request an authorisation to detain a suspect on mere suspicion and, via the same warrant, deprive them of the right to counsel and the right to petition for *habeas corpus*. This could violate the non-derogable right not to be subjected to prolonged arbitrary detention. This would also constitute involuntary disappearance, which is prohibited under international law not merely because it is wrong in itself, but because it typically facilitates the violation of other non-derogable rights, in particular the right not to be tortured or even the right not to be deprived of life.[39]

After a change of government in 2015 (which occurred after an election in which the reform of Canada's anti-terrorism legislation was a plank in the victorious party's election platform), proposed amendments were put before Parliament in the form of Bill C-59, which purported to address the concerns of rights advocates. This was a long-awaited opportunity for a retrenchment of dangerous threats of the infringement of non-derogable rights that had been adopted in an overheated political atmosphere, in which further terror attacks were thought to be imminent.

Unfortunately, Bill C-59 leaves a number of these threats intact and primed for misuse in a future public order emergency. The provision of the Criminal Code that allows for preventative detention created by the Anti-terrorism Act, 2001 (and the lengthened maximum duration authorised by the Anti-terrorism Act, 2015) remain intact. Despite scholars' concerns about the possibility of the new warrant regime being used to authorise involuntary disappearance, an amendment that would explicitly specify that suspects in preventative detention have a right to counsel was rejected; the Act still fails to recognise the existence of non-derogable rights, much less specifically exempting them from the scope of the derogation warrants.[40]

Accordingly, despite the fact that there has been no terrorist attack in Canada since 2014 (and the fact that only two people were killed that year, as the wave of attacks predicted in conformity with the harbinger theory never materialised),[41] the Canadian Parliament failed to include these essential protections for non-derogable rights after a long-awaited legislative review of over-broad emergency powers legislation. To understand why, it is essential to understand how the harbinger theory also introduced fatal distortions into the public consultation on national security that preceded the drafting of Bill C-59, which accounts in part for its many inadequacies.

4. The argument that rights must be balanced against security

The Green Paper that launched the consultation process on the revision of Canada's national security legislation began with the statement that 'Canada has long dealt with terrorism threats from a diverse set of groups. Some threats resulted in tragic terrorist attacks'.[42] It concluded with a call to balance the promotion of security with the protection of rights:

> The threat of terrorism, by global and by domestic actors, is real and evolving. More people are radicalizing to violence. Some are leaving Canada to join terrorist groups overseas, while others focus their attention on Canada itself. Canadians expect the Government to keep them safe. At the same time, the Government must comply with the rights enshrined in the Charter.

There are three key claims contained in the government's argument. First, that the threat of terrorism is 'real', a term that disguises the necessity of determining how substantial it is before deciding whether Canadians should be asked to compromise any of their rights, let alone those which are non-derogable. Second, at the inauguration of the public consultation, the government stated what Canadians allegedly expect – to be kept safe by the government – despite the fact that a public consultation is meant to be the process wherein the public's expectations about the government are sought. This prefigured a fatally flawed consultation process in which the public was told what they expected of the government, by the government. Third, the government implicitly portrays Charter rights as unfortunate shackles that hinder it when it goes about its task of keeping Canadians safe (a governmental objective that is not found in the Canadian Constitution, while the rights at issue are its *raison d'être*).[43]

Framing the public consultation in this manner was necessary for the government to meet its central goal: to prevent the elimination of the regime of derogation warrants, which remained extremely unpopular with both lawyers and the public. To avoid this, the government relied heavily on one talking point: the need to 'balance' security with rights.[44] Many of the in-person events organised by Public Safety Canada were invitation only and dedicated to stakeholder groups – such as the heads of prosecution services and Chiefs of Police – who would accept and validate this key premise, owing to their personal and institutional investment in the importance of security. Most problematically, the statements of CSIS about the 'real' threat of terrorism were inevitably taken at face value.[45]

At the conclusion of its Potemkin consultation, the government commissioned a summary report from a global relations firm.[46] Predictably, its conclusions were massaged to fit what had been pre-determined by the Green Paper. The narrative the government created to protect its legislative rearguard action in support of the regime of rights-infringing warrants had two fronts: the first was the public perception of the threat of terrorism, and the second was the creation of an illusion of greater oversight and transparency.

4.1. Terrorism and CSIS: what was affirmed and what was suppressed

When considering whether there is a serious threat to the security of the nation, one should first consider the source of claims that any threat exists. The government demonstrated itself to be highly credulous throughout the public consultation process, at least when the source was Canada's 'national security institutions', presumably because of the judgment that these organisations 'are professional, responsible and effective in the work that they do'.[47]

If this glowing evaluation is accurate, then the warnings of significant danger from terrorism from CSIS and related entities should be taken seriously, although it should be noted that given that decisions about the budget and organisational clout of these agencies hinge on that assessment, whenever these agencies are called upon to make such a determination they are operating within a conflict of interest. As Upton Sinclair noted, 'it is difficult to get a man to understand something, when his livelihood depends on his not understanding it' – where the 'something' in this instance is that the dangers of terrorism have been vastly overstated.[48]

As the next two subsections will demonstrate, the government has promoted a false narrative of CSIS's professionalism and responsibility in order to promote the credibility of its conclusions, despite the fact that its most fundamental interests are in tension with its duty to produce objective threat assessments; first, it will be demonstrated that the government downplayed a number of scandals that occurred throughout CSIS's history, both early and recent; and, second, that the government ignored a breaking scandal during the consultation process, one that calls into question whether CSIS is, to some degree, creating its own evidence to bolster the harbinger theory.

4.1.1. CSIS's reliability: unprofessionalism ignored

The government's Green Paper that inaugurated the public consultation relied upon this positive evaluation of CSIS to adopt without reservation the alarmist assessments about the threat to Canada contained in the *2016 Public Report On The Terrorist Threat to Canada*,[49] which noted that 'responsibility for approving the threat level rests with the Director of CSIS'. There is no discussion of the conflict of interest that was created when the Anti-terrorism Act, 2015, transformed CSIS from an agency responsible for intelligence analysis to a fully fledged domestic counterintelligence agency performing 'disruption' operations.

That same year, the five-year budget for intelligence and security operations was increased by approximately $300,000,000, as part of a set of laddered yearly increases that will peak at $92,000,000 in 2020. In effect, in the same year that new powers were granted to CSIS owing to its assessment of terrorism predicated largely on the death of two Canadians, CSIS was placed on a budgetary track that would bring it from the status of a small intelligence analysis agency into an organisation that resembles the United Kingdom's Security Service (colloquially known as MI5).[50]

After these increases take effect, the annual budget of CSIS will be well over half a billion dollars, and it will have over 3000 employees. The annual budget of the Communication

Security Establishment (the Canadian electronic surveillance agency) is now approximately $600,000,000, after an increase of approximately 600% since 2001.[51] Given that this largesse was predicated in part on the harbinger theory, the expectation that the intelligence agencies would rebuke it runs counter to Sinclair's maxim, not to mention the proverb that a dog rarely bites the hand that feeds it. In an era of public policy marked by the retrenchment of governmental services, Canada has allowed its intelligence agencies to flourish; it has also chosen to trust them to inform the government if and when it should stop enlarging their budgets.

What is most remarkable about the glowing assessments of CSIS's ability to make a correct (yet to a great extent at least self-interested) 'threat assessment' is that it ignores a well-documented record of failure, abuse and the politicisation of intelligence. CSIS exists precisely because of the exposure by the McDonald Commission of wrongdoing by the Royal Canadian Mounted Police (RCMP)'s National Security Service, which had waged a campaign against Québec nationalists in the 1970s that included committing 400 illegal break-ins, arson, theft of party membership lists and an attempted bombing.[52]

The decision to give CSIS the power to conduct disruptive counter-terrorism operations was made after CSIS itself was involved in a number of high-profile controversies: shortly after its founding in 1984, CSIS compromised the investigation of the most serious terrorist attack in Canadian history: the bombing of Air India Flight 182 by the Sikh separatist organisation Babbar Khalsa. Ultimately, the Air India Inquiry labelled CSIS's surveillance 'ineffective' and marred by 'inexcusable' errors;[53] CSIS's misconduct extended into interference with the inquiry itself, as CSIS destroyed hundreds of hours of interviews with confidential sources, in direct opposition to orders.[54] More recently, the judiciary confirmed that CSIS was capable of not only incompetence and insubordination, but also deception: in 2015, the Federal Court found that CSIS had breached its duty of candour – more prosaically, CSIS had failed to tell the court that it was seeking warrants that it had no legal basis to request.[55]

In 2017, the professionalism of CSIS operatives was again called into serious doubt by a lawsuit seeking $35,000,000 that was brought by former intelligence officers and analysts, who claimed CSIS was 'a toxic workplace ... [and] accuse the spy agency of Islamophobia, racism, and homophobia'.[56] These are very serious allegations, insofar as CSIS is charged with determining whether Muslims and other communities of racialised Canadians constitute a terrorist threat: racism and Islamophobia are closely correlated with inaccurate assessments about the danger posed by members of those groups.[57] The lawsuit was pending throughout the 2017 public consultation on national security, during which the government engaged in stalling tactics that produced a stern judicial rebuke, as the judge told lawyers for CSIS that they cannot 'act as if the Rules do not apply. This is not acceptable ... there is something unusual happening here, and I am polite in my language'.[58]

Despite being highly irregular, these delays were not surprising, given the fact that the government was relying on CSIS's purportedly sterling professionalism to bolster its threat assessment – at the very time the pleadings it did not reply to in a timely manner painted a 'graphic portrait of a spy service-cum-frat house rife with copious on-the-job drinking'.[59] Journalist Andrew Mitrovoica argued, 'this lawsuit ... augments a growing body of evidence that strongly suggests intelligence-gathering by CSIS ... is driven, in part, by bigotry – especially towards Muslims. This, in turn, is distorting their judgment of who actually poses a real threat or not'.[60]

After the public consultation was concluded, and shortly after CSIS was rebuked for failing to respond in a timely manner to the allegations raised in the lawsuit, the government settled the lawsuit. The terms of the settlement are confidential, but it is telling that CSIS chose to give the plaintiffs enough to convince them to accept the dismissal of the lawsuit rather than to contest its shocking allegations.[61] Despite being outrageous, these claims paled compared to what was revealed on the court records of the case against the 'Victoria Canada Day Bombers' (detailed below) which is still pending appeal. As the next section will demonstrate, the judicial findings in that case revealed that CSIS not only attempted to forestall court decisions that tarnish its image, but that it went to great lengths to promote the impression that Islamic terrorism was a serious threat to Canada – and that it had exceeded all the boundaries of ethics to further the public's acceptance of the harbinger theory just as it fought to keep the expansive powers that push up against the ultimate limits of the rule of law.

4.1.2. The Canada Day bombing plot: entrapment facilitated by CSIS?

On 1 July 2013 – Canada Day – the front pages of the nation's newspapers detailed a chilling story: a major terrorist attack in Victoria had been foiled at the last minute. Two terrorists – John Nuttall and Amanda Korody, recent converts to Islam – had planted pressure cooker bombs (similar to those used by the Boston Marathon bombers in 2013) at a park where the shrapnel would have killed and injured hundreds during the celebration of the national holiday. It would only be four years later that the truth was revealed in a ruling of the Supreme Court of British Columbia: there had indeed been a conspiracy, but the participants had been the RCMP and CSIS, who had entrapped two pathetic individuals into a plot that appears tailor-made to convince Canadians of the need for vigilance against Islamic terrorism.

The two alleged terrorists – who were granted a permanent stay of proceedings after a judicial finding of entrapment in 2016 – were particularly vulnerable people. Both were heroin addicts who cycled between precarious living arrangements and homelessness. One had a long record of petty crime and was believed by local social workers and police to be developmentally delayed.[62] This was known to the undercover officers who were later found to have entrapped him.[63] It is difficult to overstate how hapless these suspects were: one journalistic account of the court's ruling notes that 'they didn't know when Canada Day was and didn't have enough money to take the ferry to Victoria or rent a motel room once they got there. That was provided by the Mounties'.[64]

The court's ruling excoriated the RCMP officers who subjected these vulnerable people to an egregious example of the controversial 'Mr. Big' sting technique, in which undercover officers befriend, impress, and manipulate suspects. This method was subjected to the criticism of a unanimous Supreme Court of Canada a year later:[65] in the 2016 entrapment ruling, the court noted that 'the police conduct must be viewed as egregious ... the world has enough terrorists. We do not need the police to create more out of marginalized people who have neither the capacity nor sufficient motivation to do it themselves'.[66]

While undercover RCMP officers took the lead in entrapping the suspects, CSIS played a shadowy role in manufacturing this outrage. In November 2012, an RCMP report about one of the suspects was passed along to CSIS; it had been generated by a procedure that led to the psychiatric assessment that identified the suspect as developmentally delayed. At some point between 2 November 2012 and 21 January 2013, CSIS concluded that this suspect was a threat to public safety, despite the fact that the only basis for that conclusion was a report that stated his mental capabilities were severely limited.[67] On 7 February 2013, CSIS released an advisory letter to the RCMP that the suspect had been attempting to purchase potassium nitrate.

The judge noted that the RCMP did not follow up on this particular allegation, which was allegedly the reason why CSIS believed the suspect was a threat to public safety:

> There was never any scenario designed to elicit Mr Nuttall's knowledge about the use of potassium nitrate in explosives .... The RCMP did not otherwise corroborate or seek to corroborate the information contained in the advisory letter. [A log of the suspects' calls] showed no telephone contact with nurseries or pharmacies where Mr Nuttall might have attempted to purchase potassium nitrate. At no time did the RCMP monitor the defendants' use of the Internet to determine if they were communicating with terrorists on social media.[68]

All this is perplexing, unless the police suspected that this allegation would not withstand scrutiny, and that the purpose of CSIS's tip had been to identify an ideal subject for entrapment rather than a genuine threat.

It should be noted that this ruling, which raises serious questions about CSIS's credibility in identifying threats to Canada, was released shortly before the public consultation on national security: it is shocking that the government saw fit to found its claim that Canadians' rights needed to be balanced against its need to protect them against threats – as assessed by CSIS – on an explicit endorsement of CSIS as 'professional, responsible and effective in the work that they do' precisely when the former analysts' lawsuit alleging a toxic work environment and a court ruling on entrapment of terrorism suspects had just revealed precisely the opposite. If the harbinger theory is accepted without question, and the intelligence agencies provide continual reinforcement of the need to prioritise security over rights, the 'balance' between these two will consistently tip towards security. Non-derogabilty and the rule of law itself cannot survive multiple iterations of this process.

5. Conclusion

Non-derogable rights are an integral part of the concept of the rule of law that was instantiated into the new regime of international human rights after the Second World War. These rights, which are also integrated into the domestic constitutional order of many states, are now under serious pressure during what is represented as an era defined by transnational terrorism.

The principal conceptual threat to the concept of non-derogability is the harbinger theory, which holds that existential threats to the state are omnipresent and only prevented from being realised by the thin blue line of state security, who obtain powers that push up against the edges of what is permissible in a rule-of-law state. Given the reflexive acceptance of the harbinger theory, even minor terror attacks (or other criminal matters that can plausibly be represented as Islamic terrorism) are frequently sufficient to catalyse expansive and highly problematic emergency powers.

In the political environment defined by the harbinger theory and the overbroad conclusions that follow from minor terrorist attacks, governments frequently adopt the stance that rights – implicitly, even those which are non-derogable – must be balanced against the demand for security. What frequently passes unobserved is that this 'balance' is never fairly struck. In order to assess what should be placed on one side of the scale, governments turn to the intelligence agencies, which are accorded substantial trust despite the fact that when evaluating the threat of terrorism they are arguably performing the most self-interested calculation one could ask of them.

Too often, intelligence agencies have exploited this trust to operate out of self-interest, seizing the opportunity to operate with impunity, to suppress evidence of their own misconduct, and to even manufacture evidence that reinforces the government's and the public's adherence to the harbinger theory. This conflict of interest means that national security legislation will always be a one-way ratchet: rights will always suffer against the perceived need for repressive measures. Non-derogable rights will only survive if the assumptions underlying the harbinger theory are challenged and the intelligence agencies are removed from a central role in reinforcing it.

Notes

1. Attorney-General Eric H. Holder, Jr., Letter of 4 March 2013 to the Honorable Ron Paul, https://web.archive.org/web/20130309221652/http://www.paul.senate.gov/files/documents/BrennanHolderResponse.pdf.
2. United Nations Committee Against Torture, 'Concluding Observations on the Combined Third to Fifth Periodic Reports of the United States of America', para. 17, CAT/C/USA/CO/3-5.
3. See e.g. The SS 'Wimbledon', United Kingdom and ors v Germany, Judgment, (1923) PCIJ Series A no 1, ICGJ 235 (PCIJ 1923), 17 August 1923, League of Nations (historical) [LoN]; Permanent Court of International Justice (historical) [PCIJ].
4. See generally George W. Baer, *Test Case; Italy, Ethiopia, and the League of Nations* (Ann Arbor, Michigan: Hoover Press, 1976).
5. See e.g. Article 53 of the Vienna Convention on the Law of Treaties, UN Doc. A/CONF.39/27 (1969), reprinted in *American Journal of International Law*' 63 (1969): 875–903.
6. UN Commission on Human Rights, The Siracusa Principles on the Limitation and Derogation Provisions in the International Covenant on Civil and Political Rights, 28 September 1984, E/CN.4/1985/4 (hereafter Siracusa Principles).
7. See note verbale dated 24 August 1984 from the Permanent Representative of the Netherlands to the United Nations Office at Geneva addressed to the Secretary-General, E/CN.4/1985/4, 28 September 1984.
8. Siracusa Principles, *supra* note 6, ss. 39.
9. United States v. Carl Krauch, VIII Trials of War Criminals Before the Nuremberg Military Tribunals Under Control Council Law No. 10 1081 (1950) [The Farben Case], 1137–8.
10. Ben Saul, *Defining Terrorism in International Law* (Oxford, UK: Oxford University Press, 2006), 3.
11. Sami Zeidan, 'Desperately Seeking Definition: The International Community''s Quest for Identifying the Specter of Terrorism', *Cornell International Law Journal* 36 (2004): 491–92.
12. Ariel Heryanto, *State Terrorism and Political Identity in Indonesia: Fatally Belonging* (New York, NY: Routledge, 2006), 161.
13. Remarks of Ronald Reagan at the at the Annual Dinner of the Conservative Political Action Conference, 1 March 1985.
14. The Republic of Nicaragua v. The United States of America, 1986 I.C.J. 14 (9).
15. Stephen Chapman, 'Contra Atrocities and US Policy Toward Nicaragua', *Chicago Tribune*, 17 May 1987.
16. President Bush, Address to a Joint Session of Congress, 20 September 2001.
17. Stockholm International Peace Research Institute, 'SIPRI Yearbook 2007', p. 636.

18. Robert Diab, *The Harbinger Theory: How the Post-9/11 Emergency Became Permanent and the Case for Reform* (Oxford, UK: Oxford University Press, 2015), 99–100.
19. See generally Ryan Alford, *Permanent State of Emergency: Unchecked Executive Power and the Demise of the Rule of Law* (New York, NY: McGill-Queen's University Press, 2017).
20. Diab, *supra* note 16, 42.
21. 'In October 2005, the chief of CTC's CBRN (Chemical, Biological, Radiological, and Nuclear) Group wrote, under the heading, "Don't Put All Your Uranium in One Bucket": "Jose Padilla: we'll never be able to successfully expunge Padilla and the "dirty bomb" plot from the lore of disruption, but once again I'd like to go on the record that Padilla admitted that the only reason he came up with the so-called "dirty bomb" was that he wanted to get out of Afghanistan and figured that if he came up with something spectacular, they'd finance him. Even KSM says Padilla had a screw loose .... Anyone who believes you can build a [nuclear device] by "putting uranium in buckets and spinning them clockwise over your head to separate the uranium" is not going to advance al-Qaida's nuclear capabilities"". Stephen Ricard, 'More Questions for Gina Haspel: The Record of False CIA Claims about Torture's "'Efficacy"', *Just Security*, https://www.justsecurity.org/55976/questions-gina-haspel-the-record-false-cia-claims-tortures-efficacy/#_ftn3.
22. Anti-Terrorism Act, S.C. 2001, c. 41.
23. Immigration and Refugee Protection Act, S.C. 2001, c. 27.
24. Colleen Bell, 'Subject to Exception: Security Certificates, National Security and Canada"s Role in the War on Terror', *Canadian Journal of Law and Society* 21 (2006): 63.
25. Immigration and Refugee Protection Act, Section 34(1).
26. CBC News Online, 'Indepth: Canadian Security: Security Certificates and Secret Evidence', CBC, February 22, 2005, http://www.cbc.ca/news/background/cdnsecurity/securitycertificates-secretevidence.html.
27. Bell, *supra* n. 24, 71.
28. As noted above, the right not be tortured is non-derogable under Article 4 of the International Covenant on Civil and Political Rights.
29. Canada (Citizenship and Immigration) v. Harkat, [2014] 2 SCR 33, 2014 SCC 37; Charkaoui v. Canada (Citizenship and Immigration), [2008] 2 SCR 326.
30. Bell, *supra* n. 24, 68; see also Jaballah, Re, [2006] FCJ No 1706 (QL), https://www.canlii.org/en/ca/fct/doc/2006/2006fc1230/2006fc1230.html?resultIndex=1.
31. Arar Commission, 'Rapport sur les événements concernant Maher Arar', http://epe.lac-bac.gc.ca/100/206/301/pco-bcp/commissions/maher_arar/07-09-13/www.ararcommission.ca/fr/Vo_II_French.pdf.
32. Maxime Deland, ""'Radicalized"' Quebecer Shot Dead After Running Down 2 Soldiers in Suspected Terrorist Attack', *Toronto Sun*, http://torontosun.com/2014/10/20/possible-terror-attack-as-soldiers-run-down-in-quebec-parking-lot/wcm/74cb0855-23bb-4782-a244-7aea18da1cf2 (accessed 30 November 2014).
33. Graeme Hamilton, 'Martin Rouleau"s Neighbours Sad but Not Surprised Over His Alleged Role in Soldier"s Death', *National Post*, 21 October 2014, http://news.nationalpost.com/2014/10/21/martin-rouleaus-neighbours-sad-but-not-surprised-over-his-alleged-role-in-soldiers-death/ (accessed 1 December 2014).
34. ""'He Said the Devil Is After Him"': What We Know About Michael Zehaf-Bibeau', *The Age*, 24 October 2014, https://www.theage.com.au/world/he-said-the-devil-is-after-him-what-we-know-about-michael-zehafbibeau-20141023-11aljl.html?skin=text-only/.
35. 'Attack on Parliament Hill: Terrorism or Mental Illness? Canadian Public Opinion Is Divided', Angus Reid, 25 November 2014, http://angusreid.org/homegrown-terrorism-radicalization-canada-overblown-serious-threat/#II.
36. Glenn Greenwald, 'Canada, at War for 13 Years, Shocked That "'A Terrorist"' Attacked Its Soldiers'. *The Intercept*, 22 October 2014, https://firstlook.org/theintercept/2014/10/22/canada-proclaiming-war-12-years-shocked-someone-attacked-soldiers/.
37. Ryan Patrick Alford, 'Bill C-51: A Threat to the Rule of Law?', *National Journal of Constitutional Law* 36 (2016): 113, 114.

38. Emergencies Act, S.C. 1988, c. 22, (4 th Supp.).
39. Siracusa Principles, *supra* note 4, ss. 59–60.
40. Ryan Alford, 'Bill C-59 and the Former Bill C-22: Compromised Oversight and Continuing Threats to Non-Derogable Rights', *University of New Brunswick Law Journal* 69 (forthcoming 2018).
41. This excluded an anti-Muslim hate crime that killed six in 2017. The perpetrator of this attack was arrested but not charged under the terrorism provisions of the Criminal Code. See Jesse Feith, 'Why No Terrorism Charges in Quebec Mosque Shooting? It Would Place Extra Burden on Prosecutors: Experts', *National Post*, Postmedia Network, 31 January 2017, http://news.nationalpost.com/news/canada/quebec-mosque-shooting-terrorism-offences-are-complex-experts-say (accessed 1 February 2017).
42. Government of Canada, *Our Security, Our Rights: National Security Green Paper*, 2016, Background Document (Ottawa: Public Safety Canada, 2016), 5, https://www.publicsafety.gc.ca/cnt/rsrcs/pblctns/ntnl-scrt-grn-ppr-2016-bckgrndr/index-en.aspx.
43. The Supreme Court has yet to adopt the position that section 7 imposes a positive duty on the government to take measures that would preserve or protect members of the public, as was articulated in the dissent of Arbour J. in *Gosselin v. Quebec (AG)*, [2002] 4 SCR 429.
44. House of Commons, Standing Committee on Public Safety and National Security, *Protecting Canadians and Their Rights: A New Road Map for Canada's National Security*, May 2017, Chair: Robert Oliphant, https://www.ourcommons.ca/Committees/en/SECU/StudyActivitystudyActivityId=8988648.
45. Alford, 'Bill C-51', *supra* note 37.
46. Public Safety Canada, *National Security Consultations: What We Learned Report*, by Hill & Knowlton Strategies (Ottawa: Public Safety Canada, 2017), https://www.publicsafety.gc.ca/cnt/rsrcs/pblctns/2017-nsc-wwlr/2017-nsc-wwlr-en.pdf.
47. Government of Canada, "Our Security, Our Rights: National Security Green Paper, 2016", p. 5, https://www.publicsafety.gc.ca/cnt/rsrcs/pblctns/ntnl-scrt-grn-ppr-2016-bckgrndr/ntnl-scrt-grn-ppr-2016-bckgrndr-en.pdf.
48. Upton Sinclair, I, *Candidate for Governor: And How I Got Licked* (Berkeley: University of California Press, 1994), 109.
49. Public Safety Canada, *2016 Public Report On The Terrorist Threat to Canada*, https://www.publicsafety.gc.ca/cnt/rsrcs/pblctns/2016-pblc-rpr-trrrst-thrt/index-en.aspx.
50. Justin Ling, 'Harper''s New Budget Is Making it Rain on Canada's Military and Spies', *Vice Magazine*, 21 April 2015, https://www.vice.com/en_ca/article/qbx4pd/harpers-new-budget-is-making-it-rain-on-canadas-military-and-spies-001.
51. Ian McLeod, 'Spies in New Glass Houses: Ottawa''s Electronic Espionage Agency Budget Blows Past CSIS, Tops $600 Million', *Ottawa Citizen*, 10 November 2016, http://nationalpost.com/news/politics/spies-in-new-glass-houses-ottawas-electronic-espionage-agency-budget-blows-past-csis-tops-600-million.
52. Commission of Inquiry Concerning Certain Activities of the RCMP, *Second Report: Freedom and Security Under the Law* (Ottawa: McDonald Commission, 1981); *Rapport de la Commission d'Enquête sur des Opérations Policières en Territoire Québécois* (Rapport Keable) (Québec: Ministère des Communications, 1981).
53. CBC News, 'Air India Case Marred by 'Inexcusable Errors', 17 June 2010, https://web.archive.org/web/20100619234239/http://www.cbc.ca/canada/story/2010/06/17/air-india017.html.
54. Andrew Mitrovica and Jeff Sallot, 'CSIS Destroyed Air-India Evidence', *The Globe and Mail*, 26 January 2000, https://www.theglobeandmail.com/news/national/csis-agent-destroyed-air-india-evidence/article4159517/.
55. See X, Re, 2014 FCA 249, 2014 CarswellNat 4344, 2014 CarswellNat 4345, [2015] 1 F.C.R. 684 (F.C.A.), leave to appeal allowed 2015 CarswellNat 182, 2015 CarswellNat 183 (S.C.C.).
56. Faisal Kutty, 'Goodale Must Investigate Racism Allegations Against CSIS', 20 July 2017, http://www.faisalkutty.com/feature_event/goodale-must-investigate-racism-allegations-against-csis.
57. Ibid.

58. Michelle Shepard, 'Judge Slams Ottawa for Delays Over $35-Million CSIS Lawsuit Alleging Workplace Islamophobia, Racism and Homophobia', *Toronto Star*, 24 October 2017, https://www.thestar.com/news/canada/2017/10/24/judge-slams-ottawa-for-delays-over-35-million-csis-lawsuit-alleging-workplace-islamophobia-racism-and-homophobia.html.
59. Andrew Mitrovica, 'Canada"s "'Untouchable"' Spies', *Al-Jazeera*, 19 July 2017, https://www.aljazeera.com/indepth/opinion/2017/07/canada-untouchable-spies-170719090810820.html.
60. Bruce Livesey, 'Is Bigotry Blinding CSIS and the RCMP – to Disastrous Effect?', *National Observer*, 14 September 2017, https://www.nationalobserver.com/2017/09/14/news/bigotry-blinding-csis-and-rcmp-disastrous-effect.
61. Michelle Shephard, 'CSIS Settles Multimillion-Dollar Lawsuit with Employees Who Claimed Workplace Islamophobia, Racism and Homophobia', *Toronto Star*, 14 December 2017, https://www.thestar.com/news/canada/2017/12/14/csis-settles-multimillion-dollar-lawsuit-with-employees-who-claimed-workplace-islamophobia-racism-and-homophobia.html.
62. R. v. Nuttall, 2016 BCSC 1404, para. 17.
63. Ibid., para. 40.
64. Thomas Walkom, 'BC Entrapment Ruling Reins in Excesses of War on Terror', *Toronto Star*, 3 August 2016.
65. See R v Hart [2014] SCC 52.
66. R. v. Nuttall, para. 832–6.
67. Ibid., para. 40–52.
68. Ibid., para. 52–6.

Disclosure statement

No potential conflict of interest was reported by the authors.

Citizenship by descent: how Canada's one-generation rule fails to comply with international legal norms

Mariette Brennan and Miriam Cohen

ABSTRACT

Since 1947, the Canadian Citizenship Act has set out the laws that determine eligibility for Canadian citizenship. Throughout the Act's various enactments, the Canadian government has recognised the right to citizenship by descent, meaning the right for a Canadian citizen to pass on his/her citizenship status to his/her child born outside of Canada. Citizenship by descent is a commonly recognised path to citizenship in many countries. Canada has recently changed its approach to citizenship by descent and has imposed a one-generation rule. This article examines the history of citizenship by descent, the current regime governing this type of citizenship acquisition and then examines how these laws comply with Canada's international legal obligations and the rule of law. Ultimately, the article argues that Canada's new approach to citizenship by descent has the potential to render children stateless, thus violating international law and the rule of law.

1. Introduction

Although Canadian Confederation occurred 150 years ago (in 1867), the concept of a 'Canadian citizen', separate and distinct from a British National, has a much shorter history. Prior to the enactment of the Canadian Citizenship Act,[1] which entered into force on 1 January 1947, a patchwork of statutes dictated basic immigration and mobility rights (that is, the rights to enter, remain in and leave Canada).[2] Recognising the great difficulty associated with defining citizenship through a variety of different statutes, the Canadian Citizenship Act sought to: 'establish clearly a basic and definite Canadian citizenship which will be the fundamental status upon which the rights and privileges of Canadians will depend'.[3] With the enactment of the Citizenship Act, Canadian citizenship became a legal reality. The creation of Canadian citizenship meant that the government had to decide to whom Canadian citizenship rights would be extended, how citizenship could be acquired and when, if at all, citizenship could be lost or revoked. Throughout the 70-year history of Canadian citizenship, the laws surrounding acquisition and revocation of citizenship have undergone myriad changes. In recent years, there has been considerable controversy surrounding the acquisition of Canadian citizenship. This article will seek to explore these controversies from an international law lens, and in particular, through an analysis of the rule of law and peremptory norms.

This article will take an innovate approach to this timely topic and focus on how, under the complex scheme set out in the Citizenship Act, Canadian citizens may be rendered stateless. While the Act has put in place safeguards to prevent the creation of stateless individuals, these precautions are grossly inadequate as they fail to fully and effectively prevent statelessness. Our claim is that the current regime imposing limitations on the acquisition of citizenship by descent are contrary to the principle of the rule of law because the current citizenship framework creates a two-tier system of Canadian citizens. Moreover, we also claim that the current citizenship framework violates Canada's international legal obligations as it allows for situations where individuals can become stateless. Prior to examining these specific arguments, we will first begin by examining citizenship acquisition.

2. Citizenship acquisition

Each state has jurisdiction to decide to whom it will grant citizenship status. The most common methods of acquiring citizenship status are through birth (being granted citizenship in the country you are born),[4] through descent (acquiring citizenship in a country by virtue of your parents' citizenship) and through naturalisation. Often states will offer a multitude of ways of acquiring citizenship. This article will briefly examine citizenship acquisition in Australia, the United Kingdom and the United States before examining the Canadian approach to citizenship acquisition.

2.1. International approaches to citizenship acquisition

Australia has multiple paths for citizenship acquisition. In addition to naturalisation,[5] a person may acquire Australian citizenship through birth in Australian jurisdiction. Unlike Canada, which grants citizenship to every individual born in its jurisdiction (a *jus soli* approach to citizenship), Australian citizenship will only be granted to a child born in its jurisdiction if either of the parents are Australian citizens or are legally permitted to live in Australia as a permanent resident.[6]

An individual may also become a citizen by descent; this means that a child of an Australian citizen born abroad is eligible for Australian citizenship. The Australian government allows multiple generations to claim citizenship by descent.[7] In order to acquire citizenship by descent, an individual must meet the government standards that prove he/she has a substantial connection to Australia.[8]

In the United Kingdom, citizenship acquisition is a blend of the Australian and Canadian methods of acquisition. Again, there are multiple pathways to obtaining British citizenship: naturalisation, descent and birth. A child born in the United Kingdom is eligible for British citizenship if either parent is a British citizen or is otherwise settled in the United Kingdom.[9] This means that, like Australia, eligibility for citizenship at birth depends on the citizenship or visa status of the parent. In terms of citizenship by descent, the United Kingdom government limits citizenship by descent to the first generation born abroad.[10]

Finally, citizenship acquisition in the United States employs methods similar to other jurisdictions; pathways to citizenship include: birth, descent and naturalisation. The United States has a very liberal approach to citizenship by birth. Virtually any person born in the United States is automatically granted citizenship.[11] The United States also allows citizenship by descent to the first generation born abroad and beyond, although there are residency requirements in order to be eligible to pass on citizenship. In short, a five-year residency requirement (including a minimum of two years after the age of 14) is required if an individual wishes to pass on his/her citizenship to his/her child born abroad.[12] This article will now turn to examine, in greater detail, Canada's approach to citizenship acquisition.

2.2. Canadian approach to citizenship acquisition

The Citizenship Act 1947 determined who would rightfully be called Canadian.[13] In short, citizenship in Canada can be acquired through naturalisation,[14] by birth on Canadian soil,[15] and through descent.[16] This article will focus on the rights of citizenship acquisition by descent, particularly the historical evolution of this right, its current application and the legality of these provisions.

Acquisition of Canadian citizenship by descent (that is, citizenship acquisition for foreign-born individuals by virtue of his/her parents' Canadian citizenship) was officially recognised in two separate provisions of the Citizenship Act. The first section dealt with individuals born overseas prior to the enactment of the Citizenship Act. Pursuant to section 4 (1)(b) a person who was not born in Canada prior to 1947 was considered to be a Canadian citizen if the father (or, if the child was born out of wedlock, the mother) met four criteria:

(a) Was born in Canada or on a Canadian ship and was not an alien at the time of that person's birth;
(b) Was, at the time of that person's birth, a British subject who had Canadian domicile;
(c) Was, at the time of that person's birth, a person who had been granted, or whose name was included in, a certificate of naturalisation; or

(d) Was a British subject who had his/her place of domicile in Canada for at least twenty years immediately before the 1st day of January 1947, and was not, on that date, under an order of deportation

The minor, who acquired citizenship using section 4 (1)(b), would automatically lose citizenship three years after his/her 21st birthday unless he/she filed a declaration of retention of Canadian citizenship.[17]

For individuals born after January 1947, the right to citizenship by descent was granted pursuant to section 5 (1) of the Act. Under this provision, a person born outside of Canada would be a Canadian citizen if:

(a) His father, or in the case of a child born out of wedlock, his mother, was a Canadian citizen at the time of the person's birth; and
(b) The birth was registered, in accordance with the regulations, within two years after its occurrence or within such extended period as the Minister may, under the regulations, authorise in special cases.[18]

These provisions remained in place until the 1977 amendments to the Citizenship Act when the government sought to correct this overtly discriminatory provision.

In the Citizenship Act 1977, the Canadian government adopted section 5(2)(b) which specifically applied to individuals born in wedlock to Canadian mothers who were living abroad at the time of their child's birth between the periods of 1947 (when the original Citizenship Act was adopted) and 15 February 1979 (when the Citizenship Act 1977 came into force). Pursuant to this section these children, who were originally denied the right to citizenship by descent, could apply for Canadian citizenship.[19]

Additionally, the Citizenship Act 1977 continued to recognise the rights of acquisition of citizenship by descent. Pursuant to section 3(1)(b), any person born outside of Canada, after 14 February 1977, was entitled to Canadian citizenship if either parent was a Canadian citizen. Additionally, section 8 of the Citizenship Act specifically contemplated Canadian citizenship by descent for second-generation (and beyond) children who were born abroad. This meant that children who were born overseas to parents who were born overseas (yet who were Canadian by virtue of acquisition by descent) could also seek Canadian citizenship. While these 'second and subsequent generation' citizens were automatically granted citizenship, they would lose it on their 28th birthday if they did not meet the 'retention' requirements of the Act.[20]

On 17 April 2009, Bill C-37, An Act to Amend the Citizenship Act,[21] entered into force. This Bill made several significant amendments to the Citizenship Act 1977. The primary purpose of the Act was to address and rectify any historical unfairness that resulted in the loss of Canadian citizenship. For those 'lost Canadians', it was retroactively restored to the point in time at which the individual had lost citizenship or to birth, if the individual had never acquired citizenship.[22] Despite the overall beneficial nature of the 2009 amendments, there were two significant criticisms of the amendments: the failure to adequately address the need for citizenship retention by the age of 28[23] and the changes made to acquisition of citizenship by descent.

With the adoption of Bill C-37, the government limited acquisition of citizenship by descent to the first generation of Canadians born abroad.[24] This meant that section 8 of the Citizenship Act 1977, which granted citizenship to second and subsequent generations born abroad was revoked. The amendments did carve out a minor exception to this limitation: if the parent was serving abroad as an employee of the Canadian Armed Forces, the federal public administration or the public service of a province.[25] During the debates surrounding the 2009 amendments, this particular alteration to the Citizenship Act was heavily criticised. Among the most significant criticisms that were levelled against this amendment was that the result of it could render individuals stateless.[26]

The lack of an automatic right to citizenship for foreign-born children can create situations of statelessness. In the vast majority of countries,[27] if a second-generation Canadian were born in that jurisdiction, the child would not be granted citizenship in his/her birth country and would also not be eligible to receive Canadian citizenship through descent. In short, the child would be stateless. Statelessness can have significant impacts on the individual: it restricts his/her ability to travel, receive government-funded assistance programmes, secure legal employment, and so on.[28] Moreover, it has been suggested that individuals who are stateless do not share in the protective ambit cast by section 15 of the Charter.[29] The flaws of this new legislation have been identified on numerous occasions and yet the most recent round of amendments to the Citizenship Act have failed to adequately rectify this problem.[30]

Since the 2009 amendments, there have been two other significant amendments (or attempts at amendments) to the Citizenship Act. The first round of widespread amendments occurred with the enactment of Bill C-24, Strengthening Canadian Citizenship Act and the second round, Bill C-6, An Act to amend the Citizenship Act and to make consequential amendments to another Act,[31] which repeals many of the 2014 amendments. The 2014 changes (that is, through Bill C-24) primarily focused on increasing grounds of revocation and changed acquisition requirements for those acquiring citizenship through naturalisation. These latter changes centred on increasing the length of Canadian residency prior to applying for citizenship[32] and language proficiency requirements[33] among other changes.[34] The amendments also barred certain individuals from being able to acquire citizenship.[35] In terms of acquisition of citizenship, Bill C-6 reduces the length of the residency requirement required for a person before applying for citizenship and reduces language proficiency to all applicants between the ages of 18 and 54.[36] In addition to these changes, Bill C-6 did attempt to address some of the concerns surrounding the limitations placed on the acquisition of citizenship through descent. Section 5(4) states that 'the Minister may, in his or her discretion, grant citizenship to any person to alleviate cases of statelessness or of special and unusual hardship or to reward services of an exceptional value to Canada'; however, the decision regarding statelessness still rests solely on the Minister's discretion and is not a guarantee that the individual will be granted citizenship.

3. The creation of the stateless individual through limitations on Canadian citizenship acquisition

As discussed in Part I, this article focuses on Canadian citizenship laws from the perspective of citizenship by descent and its impact on statelessness, in light of Canada's international obligations. The goal of the article is to tackle the reasons why, as it currently stands, rules on the acquisition of Canadian citizenship by descent to children born abroad of Canadian parents also born abroad (the 'first generation rule') are at odds with Canada's obligations under international law regarding reduction of statelessness. This section of the article focuses on the phenomenon of statelessness, how current Canadian citizenship laws put individuals at jeopardy of becoming stateless and its implications from an international law perspective. We first overview nationality or citizenship under international law,[37] then we address Canada's international legal obligations and we finally discuss the 'first generation rule' through the lens of international legal norms and the rule of law.

3.1. Nationality under international law

A number of international conventions address nationality (citizenship) under international law. The right to a nationality is guaranteed under the Universal Declaration of Human Rights (UDHR) as well as the right not to be arbitrarily deprived of nationality.[38] Unfortunately, the UDHR fails to provide guidance on how to interpret arbitrariness.[39] In addition to the UDHR, the International Covenant on Civil and Political

Rights states, in regard to nationality, that '[e]very child has the right to acquire nationality'.[40] Moreover, the Convention on the Rights of the Child provides that a child shall have the right from birth 'to acquire a nationality'. Significantly for the discussion in this article, Article 7(2) stipulates that,

> States Parties shall ensure the implementation of these rights in accordance with their national law and their obligations under the relevant international instruments in this field, in particular where the child would otherwise be stateless.[41]

Beyond these conventions, dealing with the right to nationality more generally, nationality is also addressed through the lens of the prohibition of discrimination. In fact, the International Convention on the Elimination of All Forms of Racial Discrimination guarantees to all equality in the enjoyment of the right to a nationality without distinction as to race, colour or national origin.[42] Canada is a state party to all these conventions.

Other than these general guarantees, the conventions do not absolutely preclude revocation of citizenship or impose rules on when to grant citizenship. A general characteristic of these conventions is that specific matters of citizenship and nationality are largely left within the purview of domestic law, for states to decide how to legislate on these matters. For example, the 1930 Hague Convention on Certain Questions Relating to the Conflict of Nationality Law states that '[i]t is for each State to determine under its own law who are its nationals'.[43] The International Court of Justice also affirmed in the infamous *Nottebohm* case that nationality is a matter falling within each sovereign state's domestic law.[44]

This panorama is, nevertheless, changing in this regard with the operation of human rights conventions and increased awareness of the issue of statelessness, which can be caused by states' laws on revocation and acquisition of citizenship. As Sir Hersch Lauterpacht stated:

> [i]n the past, nationality was viewed as a privilege of somewhat rigid and almost mystical character conferred by the state. It is now increasingly regarded as an instrument for securing the rights of the individual in the national and international spheres.[45]

For example, the Inter-American Court of Human rights has stated, with regard to states' discretion to craft nationality laws and the risk of statelessness:

> The determination of who has a right to be a national continues to fall within a State's domestic jurisdiction. However, its discretional authority in this regard is gradually being restricted with the evolution of international law, in order to ensure a better protection of the individual in the face of arbitrary acts of States. Thus, at the current stage of the development of international human rights law, this authority of the States is limited, on the one hand, by their obligation to provide individuals with the equal and effective protection of the law and, on the other hand, by their obligation to prevent, avoid and reduce statelessness.[46]

3.1.1. Jus cogens *standards and the right to nationality*

Peremptory or *jus cogens* standards are a 'general principle of law based on the near universal commitment of national legal systems to insulating certain basic norms from derogation'.[47] There is still much uncertainty about the status of *jus cogens* standards under international law, and while numerous international conventions recognise the right to nationality, it does not seem that this right has reached the level of a peremptory norm.

3.2. Statelessness under international law

International law addresses the issue of statelessness in specific conventions. Considering how the issue of statelessness is intertwined with the right to a nationality and domestic citizenship laws, this article now turns to the particular question of statelessness under international law and in the Canadian context.

Statelessness is the object of specific United Nations conventions that complement the texts discussed above concerning the right to a nationality under international law. These are the 1954 Convention relating to the Status of Stateless Persons[48] and the 1961 Convention on the Reduction of Statelessness,[49] which together provide the foundational international legal framework addressing statelessness.

The 1954 UN Convention sets out the international legal framework to address statelessness. It includes the standards of protection for stateless persons. The 1954 UN Convention provides that a 'stateless person' is 'a person who is not considered as a national by any State under the operation of its law'.[50]

Canada is not a party to this convention. It has been reported that the 'decision not to accede to the 1954 Convention is based, in part, on Canada's belief that its legal framework provides sufficient protection for the rights of stateless persons and that accession is redundant and unnecessary'.[51] Despite this, a 2012 report commissioned by the United Nations High Commissioner for Refugees (UNHCR) Canada concluded that, 'current federal legal mechanisms are insufficient to protect stateless persons in Canada'.[52]

The 1961 UN Convention deals with citizenship conferral and non-withdrawal so as to reduce statelessness. This convention establishes a legal framework with obligations on states parties to establish safeguards in their laws to prevent statelessness, both at birth and later. Canada has been a party to this convention since 9 July 1978 and upon accession it did not enter any reservations.[53] As a party to this convention, Canada has obligations to ensure that its domestic laws (that is, mainly the Citizenship Act) are in conformity with its terms and thus effectively reduce instances of statelessness.[54]

The 1961 UN Convention addresses both grants of citizenship and citizenship revocation. Concerning granting citizenship at birth, Article 4 (1) provides that:

> A Contracting State shall grant its nationality to a person, not born in the territory of a Contracting State, who would otherwise be stateless, if the nationality of one of his parents at the time of the person's birth was that of that State. If his parents did not possess the same nationality at the time of his birth, the question whether the nationality of the person concerned should follow that of the father or that of the mother shall be determined by the national law of such Contracting State. Nationality granted in accordance with the provisions of this paragraph shall be granted:

(a) at birth, by operation of law, or
(b) upon an application being lodged with the appropriate authority, by or on behalf of the person concerned, in the manner prescribed by the national law. Subject to the provisions of paragraph 2 of this Article, no such application may be rejected.

Concerning the granting of citizenship at birth, an expert meeting convened by the UNHCR on the 1961 UN Convention reported that:

> The right of every child to acquire a nationality, as set out in CRC Article 7 and the principle of the best interest of the child contained in CRC Article 3, create a strong presumption that Contracting States should provide for automatic acquisition of their nationality at birth to an otherwise stateless child born abroad to one of its nationals. In cases where Contracting States require an application procedure, international human rights law, in particular the CRC, obliges States to accept such applications as soon as possible after birth.[55]

Stateless people are very vulnerable, without a right in practice to have rights and protection in any country. In particular, stateless children face systemic barriers to social assistance, health care and education.[56] While the right to nationality appears in various international conventions to which Canada is a party, and the 1961 UN Convention on reduction of statelessness, the current legal framework in Canada does indeed pose a real threat to creating stateless children through the 'first generation rule'. In light of this risk, and taking into account Canada's international obligation, in its recent report, the Canadian Centre on Statelessness recommended abolishing the 'first generation rule'.[57]

3.3. Citizenship and statelessness in Canada

Citizenship in Canada is granted *jus soli* and *jus sanguinis*, which in general terms means that persons born in Canada as well as those born abroad (to Canadian parents) are granted Canadian citizenship.

Concerning the acquisition of citizenship by descent, as explained above, there is however a limitation on passing Canadian citizenship to second and subsequent generations of Canadians born abroad, otherwise referred to as the 'first generation rule'. These individuals, who would have normally acquired citizenship at birth, do not have citizenship because they were born outside of Canada to parents who were themselves born abroad.[58] The law provides an avenue whereby the second generation of Canadians born abroad can *apply* for Canadian citizenship if they can prove that they would otherwise be stateless, if they are under 23 and have resided in Canada for three of the four years preceding their application.[59] At first sight, this framework may seem to generally abide by the 1961 UN Convention, but it does not do away with the risk that the second generation (and beyond) of children born abroad will remain stateless for at least some time during their childhood, and will have the burden of proving the latter requirements in order to succeed in their application for citizenship.

There are very few reported court cases concerning statelessness in the Canadian context[60] and scholarship is also sparse in this field. While this article is not arguing that the government has to grant citizenship in all instances, to everyone, the 'first generation rule' under the current regime poses the risk of creating stateless individuals. A review of instruments discussed above relating to the right to a nationality and more specifically conventions on statelessness, demonstrates that citizenship – or, in international law terms, nationality – is regarded as a right under international law, even if international conventions are minimalist and leave much discretion to states to craft citizenship laws.[61] More specifically in relation to statelessness, specific conventions circumscribe instances where states may revoke or fail to grant citizenship, with a view to reducing statelessness. Authoritative interpretations also suggest that international law is concerned with how domestic laws may contribute to the creation of statelessness.[62]

There are not enough guarantees under Canadian law to protect individuals from statelessness when the 'first generation rule' is applied. This article argues that the federal government, as a minimum, should include protections that allow children born abroad to obtain Canadian citizenship automatically at birth if they would be born stateless. Moreover, the 'first generation rule', as discussed in the next section, creates two-tiers of Canadians: the first generation of Canadians born abroad and whose children are born abroad who will not have Canadian citizenship at birth, and the Canadian citizens born in Canada who do not have limitations on passing on their citizenship. Thus, both the causes as well as the consequences of statelessness are issues that Canada will need to continue to confront, especially as they relate to the grant of citizenship.

3.3.1. How to reconcile statelessness and the rule of law?

The rule of law is a concept that embraces fundamental notions that Canada adheres to as a constitutional principle. In the *Quebec Secession Reference*, the Supreme Court of Canada explained the principle of the rule of law as including:

> 'The law must be supreme over the acts of government and private persons'; it is guaranteed 'to the citizens and residents of the country a stable and ordered society in which to conduct their affairs'; and that 'the relationship between the state and the individual must be regulated by law'.[63]

Considering the concept of the rule of law, the 'first generation rule' creates two categories of citizens: those who can pass on citizenship to their decedents and those who cannot due to the place they were born. The rule of law dictates that all are equal before the law. The reality with the Citizenship Act's current provision on acquisition of citizenship does not treat all citizens equally. This contravenes fundamental international human rights treaties, to which Canada is a party, and it is contrary to the rule of law, by which Canada is governed.

The rule of law demands legislation be in place to regulate the relationship between the state and the individual. In this respect, this article argues that to adhere to the rule of law, changes to the Citizenship Act must occur for the sake of equality, the normative construction of society, and the legal relationship between state and citizen.

4. Conclusion

Citizenship laws in Canada have gone through some significant changes in the past decade, both relating to citizenship revocation and the acquisition of Canadian citizenship. Significantly, the law on the acquisition of citizenship has been modified with the result that the second generation of Canadians born abroad are not entitled to Canadian citizenship. Our contribution to the scholarly debate in this field focused on an analysis of the risks of creating stateless individuals under current citizenship provisions, through the lens of international legal norms and the rule of law.

This article reviewed the evolution of Canadian citizenship laws relating to acquisition of citizenship and the issue of statelessness under international law. While recent changes to the Canadian citizenship legal framework may seem, a first glance, to comply with international law obligations of Canada, when examined through the lens of statelessness, the picture is entirely different. We claimed in this article that Canadian laws concerning citizenship acquisition are at odds with rule of law values and pose a significant risk of creating stateless individuals, contrary to Canada's international law obligations. In short, denying second and subsequent generations of Canadians born abroad the right to citizenship by descent creates a two-tiered typology of Canadians, which denies the very notion of rule of law and equality, and creates a serious risk of statelessness.

This article concludes that reform is needed to ensure that the current legal framework is not contributing to the creation of stateless individuals. When changing or crafting citizenship laws, statelessness should not be taken lightly.

Notes

1. Canadian Citizenship Act, 1946, SC 1946, c 15 (Citizenship Act or Act).
2. See The Immigration Act, 1910, SC 1910, c 27 as revised in RSC 1927, c 93; The Naturalization Act, 1914, SC 1914, c 44 as revised in RSC 1927, c 138; and an Act to define Canadian Nationals and to provide for the Renunciation of Canadian National, SC 1921, c 4 as revised in RSC 1927, c 21.
3. 'Canadian Citizenship Act', 2nd reading, House of Commons Debates, 20th Parl, 2nd Sess, No 1 (2 April 1946), 502–10 (Hon Paul J J Martin). (Hon Paul J J Martin (Sr.), Secretary of State of Canada when he moved for the second reading on 2 April 1946 of the Bill respecting citizenship, nationality, naturalisation and status of alien.) See also *Taylor* v. *Canada (Minister of Citizenship and Immigration)*, 2007 FCA 349, [2008] 3 FCR 324 at para. 39.
4. States often limit who, even if they are born in the country, receives citizenship. This will be explained in more detail when examining individual countries.
5. See Australia, Commonwealth, Department of Immigration and Border Services, *Recent Changes to Australian Citizenship Legislation*, https://www.border.gov.au/Trav/Citi/Lear/Law-and-policy/legis-changes (Australia is in the process of amending its eligibility rules surrounding naturalisation. It is incorporating Australian values provisions, increasing residency requirements, altering English language comprehension, and so on. All of these changes are meant to strengthen and protect Australian citizenship).
6. See Australia, Commonwealth, New South Wales Government, *Temporary Residents Program* (last updated 20 November 2015), http://www.detinternational.nsw.edu.au/media-assets/trp/residency-status.pdf (if the child is born in Australia but the parent is neither a citizen nor a permanent resident, the child will be granted a temporary resident visa and will be eligible for Australian citizenship when he/she turns 10 years old, if they are still residing in the country).
7. Australia, Commonwealth, Department of Immigration and Border Protection, *Citizenship by Descent-Eligibility*, https://www.border.gov.au/Trav/Citi/pathways-processes/application-options/descent/eligibility.
8. The Australian government requires a person (other than those eligible as a first-born abroad generation) to have resided for two years in Australia prior to being able to pass on his/her citizenship by descent. Ibid.
9. British Nationality Act, 1981 (UK) c 61, s 1.1. See also UK, UK Visas and Immigration, *Nationality Instructions*, 1 (2 December 2013), Ch. 1, https://www.gov.uk/government/collections/nationality-instructions-volume-1.
10. British Nationality Act, 1981 (UK) c 61, s 1.1. See also UK Visas and Immigration, *Nationality Instructions*, Ch. 4. Similar to Canadian law, the United Kingdom does allow an exception if the child was born abroad because the parent was working or employed with the United Kingdom government (including its armed forces).
11. Jon Feere, 'Birthright Citizenship in the United States: A Global Comparison' (Center for Immigration Studies, August 2010), 15, Table 1, http://www.cis.org/sites/cis.org/files/articles/2010/birthright.pdf.
12. US, US Citizenship and Immigration Services, *Citizenship Through Parents*, 10 November 2015, https://www.uscis.gov/us-citizenship/citizenship-through-parents.

13. *Taylor v. Canada (Minister of Citizenship and Immigration)*, 2007 FCA 349, [2008] 3 FCR 324 at para. 42 (*Taylor*). 'The Citizenship Act was designed to be an all-encompassing law on citizenship and was meant to deal with all possible scenarios of who had a right to Canadian citizenship. The breadth and significance of this piece of legislation have since been recognised: "The 1947 Act is a complete code for Canadian citizenship. It deals with persons born before January 1, 1947, as well as with those born thereafter. It deals with persons born in Canada as well as with those born outside Canada. It determines which of these persons are Canadian citizens as of right, and with respect to those persons who are Canadian citizens as of right, it determines which may apply for a grant of Canadian citizenship, and how, and subject to what requirements. The 1947 Act also determines when or how Canadian citizens lost their citizenship."'
14. Citizenship Act, RSC 1985, c C-29, s 5 (Citizenship Act, 1985) (in order to acquire citizenship through naturalisation, an individual must meet the requirements of section 5 of the Citizenship Act, 1985). See generally Jamie Chai Yun Liew and Donald Galloway, *Immigration Law*, 2nd ed. (Toronto: Irwin Law, 2015), 445.
15. Ibid., s 3(1)(a) (individuals born on Canadian soil are granted citizenship pursuant to section 3 (1) (a) of the Citizenship Act). But see Ibid., s 3(2) (there are exceptions to this for individuals whose parents reside in Canada for the purposes of diplomatic services). See generally Liew and Galloway, *Immigration Law*, 439–40.
16. Acquisition of citizenship by descent means that any child born to a Canadian citizen automatically has a right to become a Canadian citizen, even if that child has never resided in or even visited Canada. See Citizenship Act, s 4; Citizenship Act, 1985, at s 3(1)(b) (the right to citizenship by descent is also granted in section 3 (1)(b) of the current Citizenship Act, 1985). See generally Liew and Galloway, *Immigration Law*, 440–45.
17. Citizenship Act, s 4(2) (this retention provision underwent a series of changes, but the net result was always the same: if the individual did not fulfil the statutory requirements of retention, he/she would lose his/her citizenship). See also Henry Chang, 'Canadian Citizenship by Birth Abroad', *Chang and Boos' Canada – U.S. Immigration Law Center* (blog), 29 June 2009, http://americanlaw.com/canadiancitizenshipbirthabroad.html.
18. Citizenship Act, s 4(3) (pursuant to section 4(3), the government allowed registration under this provision until 14 August 2004 (for all individuals who were entitled to make a citizenship claim under the provision); this meant that an individual who was born in 1950, if they met the criteria of the section, had until 14 August 2004 to register his/her citizenship. After that date, the government would no longer grant citizenship through this section).
19. Citizenship Act, SC 1974-75-76, c 108, s 5(2)(b) (Citizenship Act, 1977).
20. The retention requirements were not particularly arduous; the individual had to: (1) make an application to retain citizenship and (2) be 'registered as a Canadian citizen and either reside in Canada for a period of at least one year immediately preceding the date of application or established a substantial connection with Canada'. See section 8 of the Citizenship Act, 1977 (regulations defined a 'substantial connection' as: 'the person has been employed, for at least two of the four years immediately preceding the date of his application, in the public service of Canada or of a province or as a member of the Canadian forces of the Royal Canadian Mounted Police or as a Canadian representative to the United Nations or one of its affiliated agencies; or [t]he person has an adequate knowledge of one of the official languages of Canada, and the responsibilities and privileges of citizenship, determined in accordance with the criteria set out in the regulations, and since attaining the age of fourteen years of age, has spent more than one year in Canada with a parent, brother, sister, aunt, uncle or grandparent or in attendance at a recognized secondary or post-secondary educational institution').
21. According to the amendments, anyone who meets any of the five new proposed grounds of citizenship are considered citizens: 1. 'A person lost citizenship for any reason other the three prohibited reasons (renunciation of citizenship; revocation for false representation, fraud or concealment of material circumstances; or failure to retain citizenship by that age of 28 (for second and subsequent generation Canadians born abroad)'; 2. 'A person was born abroad

before 15 February 1977 to a Canadian parent but never became a citizen'; 3. 'A person was born abroad before February 1977 to a Canadian parent and who did not become a citizen by descent but went through the process to "immigrate" to Canada and become a Canadian citizen through naturalization'; 4. 'A person had been a citizen other than by way of grant, ceased to be citizen for a reason other than one of the three prohibited reasons listed in situation 1 above, but regained citizenship under the current Citizenship Act, 1985'; and, 5. 'A person had been a citizen other than by way of grant, ceased to be a citizen for a reason other than of the three prohibited reasons listed in situation 1, above, but resumed his or her Canadian citizenship under a provision from prior legislation'. The changes were adopted into the Citizenship Act, 1985, through section 3(1)(f)–(j). See also Bill C-37, An Act to amend the Citizenship Act, 2nd Sess, 41st Parl, 2014, http://www.lop.parl.gc.ca/About/Parliament/LegislativeSummaries/bills_ls.asp?Language=E&ls=C37&Mode=1&Parl=39&Ses=2&source=library_prb (Revised Bill C-37 by Penny Becklum of the Law and Government Division on the 20 February 2014) (Bill-37).

22. Citizenship and Immigration Canada, 'History of Citizenship Legislation', 6 July 2015, http://www.cic.gc.ca/english/resources/tools/cit/overview/hist.asp (according to the background documents for Bill C-37, there are four distinct groups of 'lost Canadians': 1. 'People Naturalized to Canada who subsequently lived outside the country for more than 10 years prior to 1967'; 2. 'People born abroad to a Canadian parent prior to the enactment of the Citizenship Act, 1977; 3. People who lost citizenship because they (or their parent) became a citizen of another country during the period of 1 January 1947 and 15 February 1977'; and, 4. 'Second and subsequent generation Canadians born abroad since the Citizenship Act, 1977'. This last group of individuals have not necessarily lost citizenship but are at risk of losing citizenship if they fail to take the necessary steps to retain citizenship by their 28th birthday. While many so-called 'lost Canadians' officially became citizens in 2009 (due to legislative amendments), those 'who were born before the Canadian *Citizenship Act* took effect [in] ... 1947 ... as well as ... their children who were born outside Canada in the first generation' did not obtain the benefit of the 2009 amendments); 'As Many "Lost Canadians" Gain Citizenship, Others Are Left in Limbo', *CBC News*, 17 April 2009, http://www.cbc.ca/news/canada/as-many-lost-canadians-gain-citizenship-others-are-left-in-limbo-1.786957 (this oversight was corrected with the enactment of the Strengthening Canadian Citizenship Act. This new Act is responsible for granting citizenship to an estimated 95% of the remaining 'lost Canadians'). See also Bill C-37, s 3(1)(f)-3(7)(d).
23. See Nicholas Keung, 'B.C. woman fights to get citizenship back after obscure rule leaves her stateless', *The Toronto Star* (28 August 2016), https://www.thestar.com/news/immigration/2016/08/28/bc-woman-fights-to-get-citizenship-back-after-obscure-rule-leaves-her-stateless.html. See also note 13. Despite all the amendments made to the Citizenship Act, the retention requirements have remained in place for all individuals who acquired citizenship through section 8.
24. Citizenship Act, 1985, s 3(3). It has been suggested that the catalyst for the 'first generation rule' was the government-funded evacuation of Canadians (many of whom had allegedly never been to Canada before) from Lebanon in the midst of the war that occurred in that region in 2006. See Lois Harder and Lyubov Zhyznomirska, 'Claims of Belonging: Recent Tales of Trouble in Canadian Citizenship', *Ethnicities* 12, no. 3 (2102): 293 at 294–300; Elke Winter, 'Impossible Citizens: Canada's "Citizenship Bonanza" and its Boundaries', *Citizenship Studies* 18, no. 1 (2014): 46 at 56; Liew and Galloway, *Immigration Law*, 441. It is reported that a general sense of unfairness arose in that individuals (sometimes referred to as 'citizens of convenience') who had no 'real connection' to Canada should be able to rely on the Canadian 'taxpayer to subsidize their flight from danger'. Harder and Zhyznomirska, 'Claims of Belonging', 294; Liew and Galloway, *Immigration Law*, 441. In light of this, the official reason for the change, according to then Minister of Citizenship and Immigration Jason Kenney, was in order to 'protect the value of Canadian citizenship for the future' (Winter, 'Impossible Citizens', 47). As such, the general sentiment behind the 'first

generation rule' was that it should be limited to 'those people who have some kind of enduring presence or commitment to Canada' (*CBC News*, 'Lost Canadians').

25. Citizenship Act, 1985, s 3(5).
26. When examining the proposed Bill C-24, the Canadian Bar Association noted that the proposed amendments failed to address the issue of statelessness created by restricting acquisition by descent to the first generation. The Canadian Bar Association called on the government to reconsider Bill C-24 to address this issue. Canadian Bar Association (National Immigration Law Section), 'Bill C-24, Strengthening Canadian Citizenship Act', Legislative Comment on Bill C-24 (2014), 28–29. The Canadian Bar Association again requested the government to review this issue when it considered Bill C-6. See Canadian Bar Association (National Immigration Law Section), 'Bill C-6, Citizenship Act Amendments', Legislative Comment on Bill C-6 (2017), 5 (CBA, 'Bill C-6'). For a general discussion on the problems associated with the amendments limiting citizenship by descent to the first generation, see Diana Mehta, 'New Citizenship Limits Baffle Canuck Dad as Baby Boy Not Considered Canadian', *The Toronto Star*, 26 September 2010, https://www.thestar.com/news/canada/2010/09/26/new_citizenship_limits_baffle_canuck_dad_as_baby_boy_not_considered_canadian.html. Those who would otherwise be Canadian citizens if not for the 'first generation rule' are entitled to apply for permanent resident status and then Canadian citizenship (pursuant to s 5 of the Citizenship Act). In short this means that these individuals, while they may be stateless when born, can apply for permanent resident status and then, after meeting the time period, can apply for citizenship. This does not rectify the problem that an individual will be left stateless for a number of years while this method of citizenship acquisition occurs.
27. It has also been noted that only 30 countries grant automatic citizenship to an individual born on their soil. The rest of the world bases citizenship on the *jus sanguinis* model that means parental citizenship rights dictate whether the child, born in the country, will receive citizenship. Feere, 'Birthright Citizenship in the United States'; Ronald Rizzo, 'Born in the USA But Not a Citizen – How the Birth Visa Can Solve Today's Immigration Challenges', *Journal of Civil Rights and Economic Development* 27, no. 2 (2013–2015): 393 at 397.
28. Amnesty International Canada, 'Bill C-24; Amnesty International's Concerns Regarding Proposed Changes to the Canadian Citizenship Act', Legislative Comment on Bill C-24 (9 June 2014), 2; Canadian Centre on Statelessness, 'Stateless Persons in Canada', http://www.statelessness.ca; Catherine Dauvergne, 'How the *Charter* has Failed Non-Citizens in Canada: Reviewing Thirty Years of Supreme Court Jurisprudence', *McGill LJ* 58, no. 3 (2013): 663. The causes and consequences will be further developed in the next section of the article.
29. Canadian Centre on Statelessness, 'Stateless Persons in Canada', http://www.statelessness.ca/who-is-stateless-in-canada.html.
30. CBA, 'Bill C-6', 13.
31. Bill C-6, An Act to amend the Citizenship Act and to make consequential amendments to another Act, 1st Sess, 42nd Parl, 2016.
32. Citizenship Act, 1985, s 5. See Citizenship and Immigration Canada, 'Archived – Strengthening Canadian Citizenship Act: A Before and After View of the Key Changes to the Citizenship Act' (5 June 2015), http://news.gc.ca/web/article-en.do?nid=985219 (specifically, prior to the new Act, one was required to reside within Canada for three out of the four years immediately preceding the application date. Furthermore, one's time spent in Canada prior to becoming a permanent resident counted towards the three-year requirement). See Brief of The Canadian Association of Refugee Lawyers, 'Bill C-24, An Act to Amend the Citizenship Act and to Make Consequential Amendments to Other Acts', Legislative Comment on Bill C-24 (5 May 2014), 4 (according to the new Act, one must reside (which is newly defined unambiguously as physical presence) in Canada 'at least 183 days in each calendar year for four out of six years' immediately preceding the application date); CIC, 'Strengthening Canadian Citizenship' (furthermore, one's time spent in Canada prior to becoming a permanent resident no longer counts towards the four-year requirement); Liew and Galloway, *Immigration Law*, 448 (closely related to the new residency requirements is the introduction

of a new (somewhat ambiguous) 'intent to reside' provision. Essentially, this obligates applicants to declare/demonstrate their intention to reside in Canada prior to receiving Canadian citizenship).

33. Citizenship Act, 1985, s 5. See also Elke Winter, 'Report on Citizenship Law: Canada' (2015) EUDO Citizenship Observatory, 17 (in a similar vein, prior to the new Act, only individuals between the ages of 18 and 54 were required to meet certain language requirements and pass a knowledge test. Following the new Act, this has been extended to individuals between the ages of 14 and 64).
34. Citizenship and Immigration Canada, 'Changes to the Citizenship Act' (8 December 2014), http://www.cic.gc.ca/english/citizenship/cit-changes.asp (other changes include a new requirement that applicants file Canadian income taxes (in accordance with the Income Tax Act), as well as 'strengthened' penalties for fraud). See also CIC, 'Strengthening Canadian Citizenship', 39 (a 'fast track' mechanism has also been created for those serving with the Canadian Armed Forces in addition to new rules making Canadian citizenship less accessible to individuals convicted of criminal offences abroad).
35. Citizenship Act, 1985, s 5 (4). See also Audrey Macklin, 'Citizenship Revocation, the Privilege to Have Rights and the Production of the Alien', *Queen's LJ* 40 (2014–2015): 1 at 29.
36. See Bill C-6.
37. In domestic legislation, the term 'citizenship' is often used, whereas under international conventions, the term 'nationality' (and its derivatives) is the norm. See in this regard, Elspeth Guild who posits 'citizen: this group is defined by national law, commonly contained in constitutions; as a term, it is most evident by its absence in international human rights conventions ... '; and 'national: in this concept there is an inference that the relationship between the individual and the state is recognised beyond the borders of the state; the national is the citizen viewed from outside the state ... '. See Elspeth Guild, *The Legal Elements of the European Identity: EU Citizenship and Migration Law* (The Hague: Kluwer Law International, 2004), 20–1. See also Daiva Stasiulis, 'The Extraordinary Statelessness of Deepan Budlakoti: The Erosion of Canadian Citizenship Through Citizenship Deprivation', *Studies in Social Justice* 11, no. 1 (2017): 1–26 at 1.
38. Universal Declaration of Human Rights, GA Res 217A (III), UNGAOR, 3rd Sess, Supp No 13, UN Doc A/810 (1948) art 15(1) (while this is not a binding treaty, it helps inform the rights in the treaties discussed in this section).
39. But see Report of the International Law Commission, UNGAOR, 67th Sess, Supp No 10, UN Doc A/67/10 (2012) 9 at 32–33, cited in Macklin, 'Citizenship Revocation', 12 (on the meaning of 'arbitrariness': 'The Commission is of the view that such a deprivation of nationality, insofar as it has no other justification than the State's desire to expel the individual, would be abusive, indeed arbitrary within the meaning of article 15, paragraph 2, of the Universal Declaration of Human Rights ... It should be clarified, however, that [draft Article 8] does not purport to limit the normal operation of legislation relating to the grant or loss of nationality; consequently, it should not be interpreted as affecting a State's right to deprive an individual of its nationality on a ground that is provided for in its legislation').
40. International Covenant on Civil and Political Rights, 19 December 1966, 999 UNTS 171 art 24 (entered into force 23 March 1976).
41. Convention on the Rights of the Child, Adopted and opened for signature, ratification and accession by General Assembly resolution 44/25 of 20 November 1989, entry into force 2 September 1990, in accordance with article 49, Article 7.
42. UN Doc A/6014, (1965) 47 at 48–9.
43. Certain Questions Relating to the Conflict of Nationality Laws, 13 April 1930, 179 LNTS 89 art 1.
44. *Nottebohm (Liechtenstein* v. *Guatemala)*, (1955), Judgment, [1955] ICJ Report 4.
45. Foreword to the first edition, in Paul Weis, *Nationality and Statelessness in International Law*, Vol. 28 (Leiden: Brill Academic Publishing, 1979).
46. *Yean and Bosico Children* v. *Dominican Republic* (2005), Judgment, Inter-Am Ct HR (Ser C), No 130 at para. 140 (emphasis added) (*Yean and Bosco*).

47. James Hathaway, *The Rights of Refugees under International Law* (Cambridge: Cambridge University Press, 2005), 28.
48. Convention relating to the Status of Stateless Persons, 28 September 1954, 360 UNTS 117 (1954 UN Convention) (adopted on 28 September 1954 by a conference of plenipotentiaries convened by Economic and Social Council resolution 526 A(XVII) of 26 April 1954. Entry into force 6 June 1960, in accordance with article 39).
49. Convention on the Reduction of Statelessness, 30 August 1961, 989 UNTS 175 (1961 UN Convention) (adopted on 30 August 1961 by a conference of plenipotentiaries which met in 1959 and reconvened in 1961 in pursuance of General Assembly resolution 896 (IX) of 4 December 1954. Entry into force 13 December 1975, in accordance with article 18).
50. 1954 UN Convention, art 1.
51. Gregg Erauw, 'Compatibility of the 1954 Convention Relating to The Status Of Stateless Persons With Canada's Legal Framework and its International Human Rights Obligations' (Report of UN High Commissioner for Refugees, 2015).
52. 'Statelessness in the Canadian Context: An Updated Discussion Paper' (Report of UN High Commissioner for Refugees, 2012), 32, http://www.refworld.org/docid/4facb7a62.html. See also generally on the 1954 UN Convention, Nicole LaViolette, 'The Principal International Human Rights Instruments to Which Canada has not Acceded' (2006) 24 Windsor YB Access Just 267 at 278.
53. 'Convention Relating to the Status of Stateless Persons' (15 May 2017) UNTC Status of Treaties, https://treaties.un.org/pages/ViewDetailsII.aspx?src=TREATY&mtdsg_no=V-3&chapter=5&Temp=mtdsg2&clang=_en.
54. See generally UNHCR, 'Statelessness in the Canadian Context', 33–4.
55. 'Summary Conclusions of the Expert Meeting on Interpreting the 1961 Statelessness Convention and Preventing Statelessness among Children' (Report of UN High Commissioner for Refugees, 2011), para. 37.
56. Canadian Centre on Statelessness and Institute on Statelessness and Inclusion Joint Submission to the Human Rights Council at the 30th Session of the Universal Periodic Review, 5 October 2017.
57. Ibid.
58. Citizenship Act, 1985, art 3(3).
59. Ibid., art 5(5).
60. One relevant case that deals with the 'first generation rule' and touches briefly on statelessness is *Kinsel* v. *Canada (Citizenship and Immigration)*, 2014 FCA 126, which we will discuss below.
61. Craig Forcese, 'A Tale of Two Citizenships: Citizenship Revocation for "Traitors and Terrorists"' (2013–2014) 39 *Queen's Law Journal* 551 at 559–561.
62. See for example, *Yean and Bosico*, para. 140.
63. See Robin Elliot, 'References, Structural Argumentation and the Organizing Principles of Canada's Constitution', *Canadian Bar Review* 80, no. 1–2 (2001): 67.

Disclosure statement

No potential conflict of interest was reported by the authors.

Securitisation, *non-refoulement* and the rule of law in Kenya: the case of Somali refugees

Oscar Gakuo Mwangi

ABSTRACT

This article adopts the securitisation theory to examine the relationship among securitisation, *non-refoulement*, a peremptory norm, and the rule of law in Kenya. The arguments raised are that Somali refugees and refugee camps predominantly occupied by Somalis are falsely, in blanket fashion, socially constructed as abetting terrorism hence existential threats to national security so that the state can prioritise the implementation of *refoulement*, a norm-violating counterterrorism measure. The rights of Somali refugees and rule of law have been violated in the context of legality and legal certainty, discretionary powers, equality before the law and non-discrimination. It is only with regard to access to justice that the rights of Somali refugees have been protected under both domestic and international law. Kenya has, therefore, derogated from the doctrine of *non-refoulement* hence violating the rule of law domestically and internationally. The conclusion offers ways of mitigating the adverse effects of securitisation on *non-refoulement* and the rule of law.

Introduction

The securitisation of Somali refugees in Kenya is largely a factor of the post 9/11 global war on terrorism. There has been a significant increase in the number of terrorist attacks in the country by the Somalia-based but transnational *Harakat Al-Shabaab Al Mujaheddin*, commonly referred to as *Al-Shabaab*, terrorist group since Kenya's military intervention in Somalia in October 2011. This has prompted Kenya's key securitising actors to, in blanket fashion, socially construct Somali refugees and the refugee camps they reside in as alleged existential threats to national security. Somali refugees have, therefore, been forcibly returned to Somalia contrary to the doctrine of *non-refoulement*, a peremptory norm. This article pays attention to securitisation, *non-refoulement*, and the rule of law in Kenya. The first section examines the conceptual relationship among securitisation, *non-refoulement* and the rule of law so as to provide a framework of analysis. The second section looks at general development of the securitisation of Somali refugees in Kenya so as to provide background information on the problem under investigation. The third section examines the relationship among the securitisation of Somali refugees, *non-refoulement* and the rule of law in Kenya. The conclusion offers recommendations on ways of mitigating the adverse effects of securitisation on *non-refoulement* and the rule of law.

Securitisation, *non-refoulement* and rule of law

This article adopts the securitisation theory as a framework to analyse the relationship among securitisation, *non-refoulement*, a peremptory norm, and the rule of law in Kenya. The concepts of peremptory norm, non-refoulement and the rule of law are, however, briefly examined before discussing the utility of securitisation theory as an analytical framework. Peremptory norms, frequently cited as *jus cogens* have a universal character whereby no state may derogate from them, despite the will of the state to do so. This extends to conflicting customary norms, general principles of international law, and treaty provisions.[1] A peremptory norm of general international law is a norm accepted and recognised by states as a whole. It is a norm from which no derogation is permitted and which can be modified only by a subsequent norm of general international law having the same character.[2] If a new peremptory norm of general international law emerges, any existing treaty which is in conflict with that norm becomes null and void.[3] *Non-refoulement* prohibits states from returning a refugee or asylum seeker to countries or territories where the person's life or freedom would be threatened on account of race, religion, nationality, membership of a particular social group, or political opinion. The doctrine is also relevant in the more general law relating to various aspects of human rights.[4] *Non-refoulement* has attained the status of a peremptory norm of international law.[5] It is stipulated in Article 33 of the 1951 Convention on the Status of Refugees (1951 Convention).[6] Exceptions to *non-refoulement* on grounds of security are stipulated in Article 33 (2). These exceptions have the potential to quash *non-refoulement*, rendering refugees vulnerable to human rights violations.[7] *Non-refoulement* obligations also exist under international and regional human rights instruments.[8] Conceptions of rule of law can be divided into two general types, thin and thick. A thin conception stresses the formal or instrumental aspects of rule of law that any legal system must possess to function effectively as a system of laws, regardless of whether the legal system is part of a democratic or non-democratic society. Thick conceptions incorporate elements of political morality such as forms of government or conceptions of human rights.[9] This article adopts the latter, wider conception which incorporates elements of democratic rule.

The essential features of securitisation theory are '(a) actors define security; (b) actors construct security; (c) security becomes "what actors make of it" through securitising speech acts; (d) the construction of security, and security itself, must be understood as a practice'.[10] Securitisation theory examines the processes that produce an 'intersubjective and socially constructed' security, whereby security or the logic of security is not actually constructed, but objectively defined. Only threats are socially constructed in the context of various issues being framed as existential threats.[11] Threats, as constructions, are based on the way those constructing interpret their reality.[12] With securitisation, security is recognised as a speech act. A speech act by a securitising actor frames an issue as an existential threat to the survival of a 'referent object' and is accepted as such by the 'audience' of the speech act.[13]

Securitisation theory pays attention to both the discursive construction of existential threats, and how this construction creates a type of politics which allows actors to disregard established norms, rules or restraints. As such, the threat of terrorism which individuals are deemed to represent supersedes particular human rights.[14] The feeling of fear that emanates from the perception that terrorism is a threat in turn influences individual and state behaviour. The state, therefore, introduces counterterrorism measures which in turn enhance individual perceptions that terrorism is a threat leading to a vicious circle of threat and response. Once the threat of terrorism is socially constructed with respect to a specific situation, the counterterrorism measures aimed at dealing with it are also socially constructed through discourse.[15] In this regard, the state's discourse on counterterrorism points out that state security actors engage in efforts to legitimise and rationalise counterterrorism measures that violate established rules and norms.[16] The securitisation theory provides an elaborate understanding of the way in which threats and threat discourses are produced, making it distinct in that it also allows potentially new interpretations of what security actually means.[17] The securitisation theory, however, has its shortcomings, especially in its focus on subjectivism. Subjectivism suggests that the possibility for misinterpretation is present in the response to any given threat.[18] Despite its shortcomings, the theory is nonetheless, highly significant as a framework that analyses the relevance of, to some degree, socially constructing terrorism and counterterrorism.

It is in the context of the foregoing arguments that this article adopts the securitisation theory as an analytical framework to examine the relationship among securitisation, *non-refoulement* and the rule of law in Kenya with regard to Somali refugees. Somali refugees and refugee camps predominantly occupied by Somalis are socially constructed as abetting terrorism, hence as existential threats to national security, so as to justify and prioritise the implementation of *refoulement*, a norm-violating counterterrorism measure. The doctrine of *non-refoulement* in Kenya has been violated, resulting in the *refoulement* of Somali refugees. Kenya has derogated from the doctrine of *non-refoulement*, a peremptory norm, hence violating the rule of law. The rule of law is examined in the context of legality and legal certainty; discretionary powers, equality before the law and non-discrimination; and access to justice.

Securitisation and *non-refoulement* of Somali refugees in Kenya

The securitisation of Somali refugees in Kenya is largely a factor of the post 9/11 global war on terrorism (GWOT). Prior to this, the securitisation was prompted by the upsurge of Somali refugees into Kenya, following the collapse and end of Siad Barrre's rule in Somalia in 1991. During the 1990s, the securitisation of Somali refugees developed around localised insecurity issues such as border insecurity, poaching and the proliferation of illegal trade in arms. Following the 11 September 2001 terrorist attacks in the United States (US) and subsequent launch of the US-led GWOT, Somali refugees became the purported 'local and regional epitome of contemporary global terrorism'.[19] The external military intervention of Ethiopia and the US against the Union of Islamic Courts (UIC) in 2006 contributed to the emergence of Islamic extremism in Somalia, prompting a new wave of refugees to Kenya. The UIC, an armed non-state actor in Somalia, had its origins in Somali clan courts and was a heterogeneous organisation based on a variety of religious traditions and political perceptions. It effectively managed to provide local-level security during its brief rule in Somalia, despite having been declared a threat to international security.[20] The Kenyan state responded by shutting the border in January 2007, citing increased insecurity in the border area and the threat of UIC militia crossing the border. Refugee registration services were suspended, leaving thousands stranded.[21] There were between 5,000 and 7,000 asylum seekers waiting on the Kenya-Somali border in urgent need of humanitarian assistance at the time of the border closure. Under normal circumstances, asylum seekers would have been registered and screened before being taken to refugee camps in Kenya.[22] The border closure provided the police the opportunity to send Somali asylum seekers back to Somalia, breaching the fundamental principle of *non-refoulement*. About 400 Somalis were *refouled* back into Somalia on the day of the border closure. The asylum seekers, mostly women and children, were loaded into trucks at Liboi in Kenya and driven to the Somalia side of the border and left without regard to any kind of accessible humanitarian assistance. Some of the Somali asylum seekers forcibly returned into Somalia had already been pre-registered with the United Nations High Commissioner for Refugees (UNHCR) in Kenya a few days before the *refoulement*.[23]

The securitisation of Somali refugees in Kenya has changed significantly due to a number of reasons mostly related to the GWOT. These include Kenya's military intervention in Somalia in October 2011, initially as Operation *Linda Nchi* and later as a military component of the peace enforcement African Union Mission in Somalia, which consequently intensified *Al-Shabaab*'s attacks in the country. It was also due to a change in Kenya's refugee policy. Since 2012 public and political concerns in Kenya over the threat posed by *Al-Shabaab* have resulted in mounting pressure for the repatriation of Somali refugees.[24] The securitisation of Somali refugees has not only been socially constructed as allegedly justified by security concerns, but also in terms of the cost of maintaining refugee camps in Kenya.[25] The social construction of Somali refugees as existential threats to national security, by securitising actors in Kenya, has largely gone unchallenged. With regard to policy change, at the end of 2012 Kenya's Department of Refugees Affairs (DRA) announced a policy requiring all registered refugees and asylum seekers in urban areas to relocate to camps as part of a plan to repatriate them to their own countries. This decision was later overturned by the High Court of Kenya. The DRA also announced that registration of asylum seekers and refugees in urban areas would be suspended. Registration has largely been closed since then, with the exception of one-off registrations for limited periods of time.[26]

On 10 November 2013, Somalia, Kenya and the UNHCR signed a Tripartite Agreement, which established a framework for the voluntary repatriation of Somali refugees in 'safety and dignity' over a three-year timeframe. Within the framework of the Tripartite Agreement, Kenya committed to ensuring that continued assistance and protection would be guaranteed to Somali refugees in the country until durable solutions had been attained within the national and international legal framework. Most Somali refugees, however, contemplated returning to Somalia as a result of negative 'push' factors in Kenya rather than positive 'pull' factors in Somalia. Such returns do not qualify as voluntary and violate the principle of *non-refoulement*. The actions of Kenya were in blatant violation of this agreement, as well as national and international law.[27]

Despite the commitments made under the Tripartite Agreement concerning humane treatment and human dignity of Somali refugees, this refugee and asylum-seeking population has been disproportionately adversely affected by counterterrorism operations in the country. Kenya has forcibly returned refugees to Somalia and Somali refugees have faced increasing harassment from the security forces in Kenya.[28] In March 2014, Kenya's Cabinet Secretary for Interior, Minister Joseph Ole Lenku, ordered all refugees residing outside Dadaab and Kakuma camps to immediately return to the camps where they are officially registered. The directive further ordered the immediate closure of all refugee registration centres in urban areas, including Nairobi.[29] In early April 2014, during 'Operation *Usalama* Watch', a counterterrorism operation, discussed later in the article, hundreds of Somali refugees were deported back to Somalia, in violation of the principle of *non-refoulement.*[30]

In April 2016 Kenya took yet another marked shift in its approach to Somali refugees. It took a number of decisive steps to discourage Somali refugees from living in the country. The first step was taken at a regional level when, on 14 April 2016, the African Union Peace and Security Council declared that the Dadaab camps were a 'legitimate security concern' and had been 'deprived of their humanitarian nature and function by the *Al-Shabaab* terrorist group'.[31] Consequently, on 29 April 2016, the government revoked *prima facie* status for Somali refugees. It also issued a directive disbanding the DRA and requiring the closure of Dadaab 'within the shortest possible period'.[32] As of 1 January 2018, there were about 488,415 refugees and asylum seekers in Kenya. The majority of these, 58.2%, originate from Somalia. The biggest refugee settlement in Kenya is the Dadaab Refugee Complex, which hosts about 234,346 refugees of whom 96% are Somali refugees. Dadaab, comprising four camps, is the largest refugee complex in the world. It is one of the largest concentrations of Somalis anywhere in the world.[33] The government appointed a taskforce to lead the repatriation process operating on two levels: the National Multi-Agency Repatriation Team in Nairobi and the Operational Refugee Repatriation team in Dadaab, with reporting lines leading to the National Security Council (NSC). A new body replacing DRA, the Refugee Affairs Secretariat (RAS), was also formed. On 31 May 2016, the Kenyan authorities issued the Report of the National Taskforce on Repatriation of Refugees from Dadaab Refugee Complex, which stated that the Tripartite Agreement had not achieved its intended purpose having recorded dismal progress due to lack of the full commitment of parties and that due to the slow pace of repatriation a decisive measure was made to hasten the repatriation and subsequent closure of Dadaab Refugee Complex, under Article 238 of the constitution of Kenya.[34] Article 238 of the constitution of Kenya outlines the principles of national security. The Tripartite Agreement, however, did not state that all Somali refugees have to return to Somalia. Nor did it include any target numbers as this would run contrary to the voluntary nature of returns.[35] Kenya's Cabinet Secretary for Interior Joseph Nkaissery consequently announced that for reasons of urgent national security and safety of Kenyans in the context of terrorist and criminal activities, Kenya had commenced the exercise of closing Dadaab refugee complex. By evoking security threats and the risk of further *Al-Shabaab* attacks, the government won domestic political support for its plans to close Dadaab. It was also perceived as an attempt by Kenya to win greater international assistance for hosting refugees, as evident when after the US pledged millions to support refugee operations, the Cabinet Secretary announced the suspension of plans to close the camp until Somalia stabilises. Notwithstanding, Kenya's political leaders continued to emphasise that the camps posed a security threat.[36] On 25 June 2016, the Tripartite Commission, comprising the Somali Minister of Foreign Affairs, Kenya's Cabinet Secretary for

Foreign Affairs, and the UNHCR High Commissioner, announced that the Dadaab camp's population size would, by the end of 2016, be reduced by 150,000 people. The process of returning refugees living in Dadaab to Somalia proceeded.[37] Kenya subsequently fixed the closure deadline of November 2016, and then extended it to May 2017.[38] In 2017, Kenya continued to pursue a policy of purported voluntary repatriation for Somali refugees in Dadaab. The pace of voluntary repatriation hastened the process that involves a number of stages, supported by the UNHCR, RAS, and international and national partners. Refugees, who opt for voluntary repatriation are provided with essential relief items and cash grants to facilitate movement. In Somalia, refugees are also provided with essential support by the UNHCR and a number of international and national partners in designated return areas.[39] These refugee support services, as discussed in the next section, have been hampered by a variety of socio-political and economic factors.

Securitisation of Somali refugees, *non-refoulement*, and the rule of law in Kenya

According to the United Nations, rule of law refers to a

> norm of governance in which all persons, institutions and entities, public and private, including the State itself, are accountable to laws that are publicly promulgated, equally enforced and independently adjudicated, and which are consistent with international human rights norms and standards.[40]

This conception is compatible with the democratic rule of law. This section examines the relationships among securitisation, *non-refoulement* and the rule of law in Kenya. The aspects of the rule of law examined are legality and legal certainty, discretionary powers, equality before the law and non-discrimination; and access to justice.

Legality and legal certainty

The relationship between legality and legal certainty and *refoulement* of Somali refugees in Kenya is examined in the context of the supremacy of the law, compliance with the law, the relationship between international law and domestic law and duty to implement the law. It is also examined in the context of non-retroactivity. The supremacy of law and compliance with the law requires that state action must be in accordance with and authorised by the law, and that the powers of the public authorities are defined by law respectively. In the case of international law, a state 'may not invoke the provisions of its internal law as justification for its failure to perform a treaty' or to respect customary international law. It applies regardless of the domestic approach to the relationship between international and domestic law. The complete domestic implementation of international law is critical. When international law is part of domestic law, it is binding law within the supremacy of law. International law, however, should not always have supremacy over domestic law.[41]

Legality and legal certainty as aspects of the rule of law are outlined in Article 2 of the constitution of Kenya. The supremacy of the law is stipulated in Article 2 (1), whereas, compliance with the law is stated in Article 2 (2).[42] In the case of the relationship between international law and domestic law, Article 2 (5) stipulates that 'The general rules of international law shall form part of the law of Kenya'[43] and Article 2 (6) states that 'Any treaty or convention ratified by Kenya shall form part of the law of Kenya under this Constitution'.[44] Article 2 (4) is crucial in that it stipulates that 'Any law, including customary law that is inconsistent with this Constitution is void to the extent of the inconsistency, and any act or omission in contravention of this Constitution is invalid'.[45] With regard to non-retroactivity, Article 116 (2) of the constitution states that 'an Act of Parliament comes into force on the fourteenth day after its publication in the Gazette, unless the Act stipulates different date on or time at which it will come into force'.[46] It is in the context of these components of aspects of legality and legal certainty that Refugees Act No. 13 of 2006 is consistent with Kenya's constitution and domestic laws as well as international laws.

Non-refoulement, as articulated in Article 33 (1) of the 1951 Convention, states that, 'No Contracting State shall expel or return ("refouler") a refugee in any manner whatsoever to the frontiers of territories where his life or freedom would be threatened on account of his race, religion, nationality, membership of a particular social group or political opinion'.[47] Article 33 (2) which pays attention to exemptions of *non-refoulement* on grounds of security is discussed later in the section that deals with discretionary powers and human rights. Article 33 (1) has been domesticated in the Kenya Refugees Act No. 13 of 2006. The Refugees Act makes provision for the recognition, protection and management of refugees and for concerned purposes. Its date of assent is 30 December 2006, while its date of commencement is 15 May 2007. The Act is in conformity with international law and international and regional treaties or conventions as stipulated in Articles 2 (5) and 2 (6) of the constitution of Kenya. Aspects of *non-refoulement* are contained in sections 18 to 21 of the Act. Section 18 of the Act that pays attention to non-return of refugees, their families or other persons states that:

> No person shall be refused entry into Kenya, expelled, extradited from Kenya or returned to any other country or subjected to any similar measure if, as a result of such refusal, expulsion, return or other measure, such person is compelled to return to or remain in a country where –

(a) the person may be subject to persecution on account of race, religion, nationality, membership of a particular social group or political opinion; or
(b) the person's life, physical integrity or liberty would be threatened on account of external aggression, occupation, foreign domination or events seriously disturbing public order in part or the whole of that country.[48]

While Section 18 of the Act is consistent and compliant with Article 33 of the 1951 Convention, with regard to compliance with the rule of law, the government of Kenya has derogated from it. Somalia is characterised as a collapsed state that has not yet had a functionally effective government since 1991. Hence any person or persons residing in Somalia is highly subjected to the conditions outlined in Sections 18 (a) and (b) of the Act. Kenya has *refouled* Somali refugees to their country of origin thereby putting them under considerable risk.

As a collapsed state Somalia cannot guarantee the sustainable safety and dignity of *refouled* refugees, since state is virtually absent in large parts of its territory. Somalia has, however, embarked on creating an enabling social, economic and political environment crucial for the sustainable return and reintegration of refugees and internally displaced persons (IDPs). Despite these efforts, a number of factors continue to threaten the humanitarian and social situation in Somalia. These include, among others, insecurity and *Al-Shabaab* presence, particularly in southern and central regions; lack of state capacities in many areas; restricted access by humanitarian and development actors; limited livelihood opportunities; lack of basic services; and poor infrastructure.[49] Additionally, grave violations against children and sexual violence against women persist in Somalia. Sexual violence is prevalent in IDP camps.[50] In this regard the security and humanitarian conditions prevailing in Somalia are not conducive for the return of refugees as this will endanger their lives. In principle, therefore, the Somali refugees should not be compulsorily returned to Somalia unless an exception applies in an individual case. The complementary protections given by international conventions such as Article 7 of the 1966 International Covenant on Civil and Political Rights (ICCPR) provide additional support for the position that the Somali refugees may not be repatriated against their will in the prevailing situation in Somalia. Protection should be offered to individuals whose refugee status has ceased, or who are subject to an exception from the *non-refoulement* principle.[51] Under conditions of state collapse, Somalia does not have the capacity to absorb the large numbers of returning refugees. In August 2016 for example, Jubaland, an autonomous region in southern Somalia, temporarily halted the return of over 1,100 Somali refugees entering the region, citing the UNHCR provision of insufficient return packages, exposing refugees to further risks; unplanned returns were contributing to the already volatile security situation; and most returnees were likely to end up in already overstretched IDP camps in the region.[52] Returns to Somalia, therefore, cannot be considered voluntary in any meaningful sense in a context of, among others, ongoing uncertainty regarding the future of refugee camps and the fate of Somali refugees who opt out of voluntary return to Somalia; and the absence of alternatives being offered to Somali refugees in Kenya. Taken together, these conditions significantly challenge the right of refugees to make truly voluntary choices or decisions based on free will, contrary to international standards.[53]

Discretionary powers, equality before the law and non-discrimination

This section examines the securitisation of Somali refugees and *non-refoulement* in the context of discretionary powers, equality before the law and non-discrimination. With regard to discretionary power, an exercise of power that leads to substantively unfair, unreasonable, irrational or oppressive decisions violates the rule of law. Executive authority should not be abused. The principle of non-discrimination requires the prohibition of any unjustified unequal treatment under the law. All persons have guaranteed equal and effective protection against discrimination on various social, economic and political grounds. Legislation must also respect the principle of equality in that it must treat similar situations equally and different situations differently and guarantee equality with respect to any ground of potential discrimination. With regard to equality before the law, the rule of law requires the universal subjection of all to the law. Equality generally should result in substantively equal treatment. To ensure that substantive equality is achieved, differences may at times be tolerated or required through equity measures, such as affirmative action, so as to redress past disadvantages or exclusion.[54]

The prevention of abuse of powers, equality before the law and non-discrimination are enshrined in the constitution of Kenya. The prevention of abuse of executive authority is stipulated in Article 129 (2), while equality before the law and freedom from discrimination are articulated in Article 21.[55] Rights and fundamental freedoms are guaranteed under Article 20.[56] In the context of legality and legal certainty, under emergency situations, the state may temporarily derogate from certain human rights on grounds of security. Emergency powers have, however, been abused by governments to restrict human rights in general. It is, therefore, essential to strictly limit the duration, circumstance and scope of such powers. State security and public safety can only be effectively secured in a democracy which fully respects the rule of law.[57] It is in this context that the government of Kenya has, on the view here, abused its executive authority contrary to constitutional provisions and international obligations on grounds of national security by securitising Somali refugees so as to implement *refoulement*, a norm-violating counter-terrorism measure.

Kenya has taken advantage of provisions contained in Sections 19 and 21 of the Refugees Act of 2006 to derogate from the principle of *non-refoulement*. These sections are derived from Article 33 (2) of the 1951 Convention which states that 'The benefit of the present provision may not, however, be claimed by a refugee whom there are reasonable grounds for regarding as a danger to the security of the country in which he is, or who, having been convicted by a final judgment of a particularly serious crime, constitutes a danger to the community of that country.'[58] In the case of Kenya's Refugees Act of 2006, Section 19 states that 'The Commissioner may withdraw the refugee status of any person where there are reasonable grounds for regarding that person as *a danger to national security or to any community of that country* (emphasis added).[59] Likewise, Section 21 of the Act states that:

(1) … the Minister may, after consultation with the Minister responsible for matters relating to immigration and internal security, order the expulsion from Kenya of any refugee or member of his family if the Minister considers the *expulsion to be necessary on the grounds of national security or public order.*
(2) Before ordering the expulsion from Kenya of any refugee or member of his family in terms of subsection (1) of this section, the Minister shall act in accordance with *the due process of law* (emphasis added).[60]

While the provisions allow for the *refoulement* of refugees on grounds of national security, the government of Kenya has abused its executive authority while doing so in the sense that it has not followed the due process of law. Following the Westgate Shopping Mall attack of 2013, the Mpeketoni attacks of 2014 and the Garissa University attack of 2015 in which 72, 60 and 152 people died respectively, Kenya's state discourse on terrorism has linked these attacks to Somali refugees and the Somali-dominated Dadaab refugee complex.[61] The state's discourse on terrorism, that constructs Somali refugees as allegedly abetting terrorism, claims, in blanket fashion, that the refugees are radicalised and aid *Al-Shabaab* in the planning and execution of terrorist attacks that lead to fatalities, casualties and the destruction of property in Kenya. Consequently, Somali refugees are erroneously framed as an existential threat not only to lives and property but more importantly to the peaceful coexistence of ethnic and religious communities, hence a threat to peace, safety and security in Kenya. Regarding refugee camps as spaces of insecurity that purportedly breed terrorism, such camps are framed as spaces that allow terrorists to exploit them for their operational efforts and as spaces that promote illicit trade in goods and weapons, hence also an existential threat to security in Kenya. The key securitising actors who have, through their public discourse and policy, constructed Somali refugees and refugee camps as existential threats are members of the country's NSC, such as the president of Kenya, the deputy president, cabinet secretary for interior, attorney-general and the inspector general national police service of Kenya.[62] The securitisation of Somali refugees has provided grounds for the state to delegitimise its role in meeting its domestic and international obligations regarding the rights of refugees. It is in this securitisation context that *refoulement* becomes part of the state's discourse on counterterrorism. The discourse on repatriation, forced relocations, and renditions of refugees as counterterrorism measures is erroneously justified on the basis of national security. Like the discourse on terrorism, the key securitising actors in the counterterrorism discourse are the aforementioned members of the NSC.[63]

The post-Kenya military intervention period in Somalia has witnessed large-scale attacks conducted by *Al-Shabaab*, hence an increase in the securitisation of Somali refugees in the country. Two notable circumstances are examined with regard to the securitisation of Somali refugees leading to Kenya's derogation from *non-refoulement*. These are Operation *Usalama* Watch of 2014 and the revocation of the *prima facie* refugee statuses of asylum seekers from Somalia in 2016. Operation *Usalama* Watch and the revocation of the *prima facie* refugee status of asylum seekers from Somalia was not only an abuse of executive authority but also abuse of the principles of equality before the law and non-discrimination as they adversely affected Somalis disproportionately. The counterterrorism operation, which began on 4 April 2014, was implemented following an attack in Mombasa on 23 March and explosions in Eastleigh, Nairobi on 31 March 2014, which killed at least ten people and injured scores of others. Security forces put up road blocks and began sweeps in the predominantly Somali area of Nairobi, indiscriminately rounding up and arresting thousands of people. The operation targeted the Somali community, including refugees and asylum seekers. It was carried out in blatant disregard for national and international law, including Kenya's 2010 constitution which reflects key provisions of international human rights instruments and refugee conventions to which Kenya is party.[64] The declared purpose of the operation was to flush out *Al-Shabaab* adherents and aliens and search for weapons, improvised explosive devices and other arms so as to detect, disrupt and deter terrorism and other organised criminal activities.[65] Out of a total number of 2,724 people screened as at 24 May 2014, more than half the number, that is 1,474 people, were ethnic Somalis. Out of a total of 481 people who had been deported as at the time, 332 were Somalis deported to Mogadishu.[66] The police considered Eastleigh a conducive environment to hide illegal immigrants and even *Al-Shabaab* operatives from Somalia. This environment was in their view conducive for the preparation and execution of the terrorist attacks.[67]

Likewise, following Kenya's policy change towards refugees in 2016 due to security concerns, the *prima facie* status of Somali refugees was revoked. In a Gazette Notice issued on 29 April 2016, whose title was 'Revocation of *Prima Facie* Refugee Status', the cabinet secretary for interior invoked the power of incumbency to revoke the *prima facie* refugee statues of asylum seekers from Somalia. The Gazette Notice stated that, 'In exercise of the powers conferred by section 3 (3) of the Refugees Act, 2006, the Cabinet Secretary for Interior and Coordination of National Government *revokes the prima facie* refugee status *of asylum seekers from Somalia …* ' (emphasis added).[68] The action specifically targeted Somali asylum seekers making the action discriminatory. By using legitimate means to do so, it is here argued, the state, via its agent the cabinet secretary, violated the principle of *non-refoulement*, constituting a breach of laws and conventions that safeguard the principle and Kenya's obligations under such international and domestic instruments to which it is a signatory.

Access to justice

This section examines the relationship between the *refoulement* of Somali refugees and access to justice in Kenya. Access to justice is examined in the context of independence and impartiality of the judiciary. In the case of fair trial, attention is paid to access to courts in the context where individuals are usually not in a position to bring judicial proceedings on their own, legal assistance is crucial and available to them, and legal aid is also provided to those who cannot afford it. It also includes the issue of whether proceedings started and judicial decisions are made without undue delay. Fair trial also pays attention to the effectiveness of judicial decisions. Judicial decisions are essential to the implementation of the constitution and legislation. The right to a fair trial and the rule of law in general would be devoid of any substance if judicial decisions were not executed.[69] Access to justice in Kenya is enshrined in Article 48 of the constitution, while the right to fair hearing is stipulated in Article 50.[70] Matters of judicial authority are enshrined in Article 159, while the independence of the judiciary is enshrined in Article 160.[71]

In the context of the relationship between securitisation of Somali refugees, *non-refoulement* and access to justice, this section refers to three notable court cases. These are Petition No. 19 of 2013 Consolidated with Petition No. 115 of 2013, Petition No. 628 of 2014 Consolidated with Petition No. 630 of 2014 and Petition No. 12 of 2015, and Constitutional Petition No. 227 of 2016. In regard to Petition No. 19 of 2013 Consolidated with Petition No. 115 of 2013, the issue raised in these consolidated petitions concerned the nature and extent of the rights and fundamental freedoms of refugees residing in urban areas in Kenya. On 18 December 2012, the government of Kenya through the DRA issued a press release and subsequently a letter dated 16 January 2013, aimed at forcibly moving all refugees residing in urban areas to refugee camps and ultimately to their home countries. The petitioners contended that the action taken by the state was a violation of Kenya's international obligations under the 1951 Convention, which has been domesticated by the Refugees Act (No. 13 of 2006), and the ICCPR. The petitioners also sought orders whose effect was to quash the government directive and stop its implementation.[72] The main issue for determination was whether the government directive captured in the press release and letter violated the constitution. The provisions of the bill of rights cited by the petitioners included Article 28 which protects the right to dignity, Article 27 which prohibits discrimination and protects the right to equality, Article 47 which entitles everyone to fair administrative action and Article 39 which protects every person's right to freedom of movement. Equally important was the fact that the law governing refugees is regulated by international law as stipulated in Article 2 (5) and (6) of the constitution.[73] In light of the findings, the court declared the government directive, contained in the press release and other correspondence, threatened the rights and fundamental freedoms of the petitioners and other refugees residing in urban areas and was a violation of the freedom of movement under Article 39, right to dignity under Article 28, the right to fair and administrative action under Article 47 (1), and violates the state's responsibility towards persons in vulnerable situations contrary to Article 21 (3). The court also declared that proposed implementation of the government directive, contained in the press release and other correspondence was a threat to the *non-refoulement* principle contained in section 18 of the Kenya's Refugees Act, 2006. The government directive contained in the press releases was thereby quashed.[74]

Petition No. 628 of 2014 Consolidated with Petition No. 630 of 2014 and Petition No. 12 of 2015 followed the enactment of the Security Laws (Amendment) Act, No. 19 of 2014. As a result of the increase in terrorist attacks in Kenya in 2014, the state enacted the Security Laws (Amendment) Act, No. 19 of 2014. The Act came into force on 22 December 2014. It amended the provisions of twenty-two other acts of parliament concerned with matters of national security, and it is these amendments that precipitated the petition. The petition challenged the constitutionality of the Act and asked the court to determine fundamental questions related to the process of the enactment of the Act and its contents.[75] This section pays attention to the amendments made to the Refugees Act of 2006 that deal with *non-refoulement.* Section 48 of the Security Laws (Amendment) Act introduced a clause that placed a ceiling on the permitted number of refugees and asylum seekers in Kenya. Section 48 16A (1) put the maximum number of refugees and asylum seekers permitted to stay in Kenya as 150,000 persons.[76] On the question whether the impugned provisions of the Security Laws (Amendment) Act were unconstitutional for violating the bill of rights, the court found that Section 48 of the Act which introduced Section 16A to the Refugee Act, 2006, was unconstitutional for violating the principle of *non-refoulement* as recognised under the 1951 United Nations Convention on the Status of Refugees which is part of the laws of Kenya by dint of Article 2 (5) and (6) of the constitution. Hence the court declared Section 48 of the Security Laws (Amendment) Act which introduced Section 16A to the Refugee Act, 2006, unconstitutional for violating the principle of *non-refoulement* as recognised by international and domestic law.[77]

With regard to Constitutional Petition No. 227 of 2016, the petition brought into sharp focus Kenya's obligations under international law, international and regional conventions, the Refugee Act of 2006, the application of the bill of rights to persons enjoying refugee status within Kenya, and the circumstances under which refugee status can legally cease to exist. The facts giving rise to this petition were, among others, that on 29 April 2016 the cabinet secretary for interior revoked the *prima facie* status of refugees of Somali origin *vide* Gazette Notice No. 46 and that the revocation effected by the Gazette Notice failed to take into consideration the country of origin information. It also lacked stakeholders' input, hence it offended the provisions of Article 47 of the constitution which requires lawful, reasonable and fair administrative action. It was also the petitioners' view that disbanding the DRA on 10 May 2016 was not preceded by public participation, and that it was *ultra vires* the powers of the minister because the said body can only be disbanded by way of a legislative process. The petitioners also claimed that equating refugees to criminals exposed them to danger of persecution and discrimination. The petition also pleaded that the threatened closure of camps and forced repatriation offended various international legal instruments protecting refugees as well as those prohibiting torture, cruelty, and degrading and inhuman treatment.[78]

The petitioners also submitted that the blanket condemnation and labelling of refugees of Somali origin as terrorists was discriminatory and violated the principle of 'individual criminality'. It was also the petitioners' case that the decision to disband Kenya's DRA did not take into account the fact that Kenya hosts refugees from several other countries and that asylum seekers would have no access to asylum procedures in contravention of Kenya's obligations under the 1951 Convention. Refugees whose identification documents had expired would have nowhere to renew their documents and the decision would undermine protection of refugees. To this extent the acts in question violated the constitution. Hence, to the petitioners, under Article 259, the constitution should be 'interpreted in a manner that promotes its purposes, values and principles; advances the rule of law, and human rights and fundamental freedoms in the Bill of Rights and permits the development of the law and contributes to good governance'.[79] Guiding the High Court decision, the judge, on 9 February 2017, stated as follows:

> ... I find no difficulty in concluding ... that the government's decision ... violates the principle of *non-refoulement* and is therefore a breach of international law, international conventions and the country's obligations under the various conventions to which it's a signatory and above all our constitution.
>
> ... the gazette notice ... specifically mentions '*revokes the prima facie refugee status of asylum seekers from Somalia ...*'
>
> In my view, the gazette notice ... to the extent that it refers to a particular community yet ... Kenya hosts refugees from several other countries amounts to discrimination and unfair treatment. ... purporting to condemn all refugees of Somali origin poses the risk of punishing the innocent.[80]

The court noted that the state of affairs in Somalia had not essentially transformed so as to warrant repatriation of refugees and also ordered the reinstatement of the DRA so as to allow the registration of Somali asylum seekers as refugees. The government of Kenya declared that it would appeal the decision, but a year later this had not yet happened. Kenya's position on the closure of Dadaab and the repatriation of refugees remains the same despite the court order. The government has latently disregarded the court ruling, largely by denying Somali refugees registration and much-needed identity documents. The RAS, which is meant to register refugees, is only primarily concerned with reducing the numbers of refugees in Dadaab refugee complex. The government also cut back its operations in the refugee complex in blatant violation of the court order. It also continued to violate its commitment during a regional Intergovernmental Authority on Development (IGAD) grouping's summit in March 2017 to continue providing asylum to Somalis.[81]

Conclusion

It has been argued that due to securitisation, Kenya has derogated from the doctrine of *non-refoulement*, disregarding the rule of law. While the country's constitution and Refugees Act of 2006 are compatible with international law, recent state action has not complied with the plight of Somali refugees in Kenya as they have been forcibly returned to Somalia under conditions of state collapse, without due process of the law. This is a threat to the physical and human security of the refugees. The government of Kenya has, on the view here, also abused its executive authority by discriminating against Somali refugees, under the guise of counterterrorism, to disregard its commitments to international humanitarian obligations. To this extent Kenya has, it is here contended, disregarded the democratic rule of law both domestically and internationally. It is only with regard to access to justice that the rights of Somali refugees have been accorded a fair trial by an independent and impartial judiciary.

Given that it is state actors that securitise Somali refugees and hence derogate from peremptory norms, it would be more appropriate for non-state actors to be actively involved in the desecuritisation processes and as such in counterterrorism efforts. Non-state actors can achieve this through informal process-oriented methods. This is already being done by non-state actors, especially in various efforts or measures such as countering violent extremism whereby civic education programmes emphasise that terrorism is not associated with any ethnic, racial and religious community but is a crime that transcends all such distinctions. By adequately demonstrating flaws or inadequacies in arguments that terrorists and terrorism are the preserve of particular social categories under prevailing circumstances, non-state actors will be in a position to delegitimise the perception that Somali refugees are terrorists on the basis of their social milieu. This will, arguably, mitigate human rights violations as the state might then not so readily be able to promulgate false narratives that seek to justify securitisation of refugees that results in derogation from the peremptory norms that protect them.

Notes

1. William E. Conklin, 'The Peremptory Norms of the International Community', *The European Journal of International Law* 23, no. 3 (2012): 837–61, 837–8, doi:10.1093/ejil/chs048.
2. United Nations (UN), Vienna Convention on the Law of Treaties 1969. Done at Vienna on 23 May 1969. Entered into force on 27 January 1980. United Nations, Treaty Series, Vol. 1155 (New York: United Nations, 2005).
3. Ibid., 22.
4. Elihu Lauterpacht and Daniel Bethlehem, *The Scope and Content of the Principle of Non-Refoulement: Opinion* (United Nations High Commissioner for Refugees (UNHCR), 2003), 89–90.
5. Alice Farmer, 'Non-Refoulement and *Jus Cogens*: Limiting Anti-Terror Measures that Threaten Refugee Protection', *Georgetown Immigration Law Journal* 23, no. 1 (2008): 2–3.
6. UNHCR, *1951 Convention Relating to the Status of Refugees* (Geneva: UNHCR, 2010), 30.
7. Farmer, 'Non-Refoulement and *Jus Cogens*', 2–3.
8. International Organization for Migration (IOM), *The IOM Handbook on Direct Assistance for Victims of Trafficking* (Geneva: International Organization for Migration, 2007), 70.
9. Randall Peerenboom, 'Human Rights and the Rule of Law: What's the Relationship?' *Georgetown Journal of International Law* 36 (2005): 828–30.
10. Felix Ciuta, 'Security and the Problem of Context: A Hermeneutical Critique of Securitisation Theory', *Review of International Studies* 35, no. 2 (2009): 301–26, 304, doi:10.1017/S0260210509008535.
11. Ciuta, 'Security and the Problem of Context', 308.
12. Michael Newell, 'The Origins of American Counterterrorism' (Institute for National Security and Counterterrorism (INSC) Working Paper Series, April 2016), 3–4.
13. Sarah Leonard, 'EU Border Security and Migration into the European Union: FRONTEX and Securitisation through Practices', *European Security* 19, no. 2 (2010): 231–54, 235, doi:10.1080/09662839.2010.526937.

14. Jonathan Bright, 'Securitisation, Terror and Control: Towards a Theory of the Breaking Point', *Review of International Studies* 38, no. 4 (2012): 861–79, 861–2, doi:10.1017/S0260210511000726.
15. Alexander Spencer, 'The Problems of Evaluating Counter-Terrorism' (UNISCI Discussion Paper, No. 12, October 2006), 15.
16. Daniela Pisoiu, 'Pragmatic Persuasion in Counter-Terrorism', *Critical Studies on Terrorism* 5, no. 3 (2012): 297–317, 298, doi:10.1080/17539153.2012.728051.
17. Ciuta, 'Security and the Problem of Context', 301; Hoger Stritzel, 'Security as Translation: Threats, Discourse, and the Politics of Localisation', *Review of International Studies* 37, no. 5 (2011): 2495–517, 2492, doi:10.1017/50260210510001579.
18. Newell, 'The Origins of American Counterterrorism', 5.
19. Jeremy Lind, Patrick Mutahi, and Marjoke Oosterom, '"Killing a Mosquito with a Hammer": Al-Shabaab Violence and State Security Responses in Kenya', *Peacebuilding* 5, no. 2 (2017): 118–35, 121, doi:10.1080/21647259.2016.1277010.
20. Oscar Mwangi, 'The Union of Islamic Courts and Security Governance in Somalia', *African Security Review*, Special Issue: The Horn of Africa 19, no. 1 (2010): 88–94, 88–90, doi:10.1080/10246021003736674.
21. Oscar Mwangi, 'State Collapse, *Al-Shabaab*, Islamism and Legitimacy in Somalia', *Politics, Religion & Ideology* 13, no. 4 (2012): 513–27, 518, doi:10.1080/21567689.2012.725659; Lind et al., 'Killing a Mosquito with a Hammer', 121.
22. Amnesty International (AI), *Kenya. Denied Refuge: The Effect of the Closure of the Kenya/Somalia Border on Thousands of Somali Asylum-Seekers and Refugees* (London: Amnesty International, 2007), 3.
23. Ibid., 3–4; Refugee Consortium of Kenya (RCK), *Asylum Under Threat: Assessing the Protection of Somali Refugees in Dadaab Refugee Camps and along the Migration Corridor* (Nairobi: Refugee Consortium of Kenya, 2012), 18.
24. AI, *Nowhere Else to Go: Forced Returns of Somali Refugees from Dadaab Camp, Kenya* (London: Amnesty International, 2016), 10.
25. Thomson Reuters Foundation, *A Review of the Legal Framework Relating to the Proposed Closure of the Dadaab Refugee Camp and Repatriation of Somali Refugees* (London: Thomson Reuters Foundation, 2017), 8–9.
26. AI, *Nowhere Else to Go*, 10–11.
27. AI, *Kenya: Waning Accountability for Justice and Human Rights, Amnesty International Submission to the UN Universal Periodic Review, January 2015* (London: Amnesty International, 2014), 4; AI, *Nowhere Else to Go*, 11–12.
28. AI, *Kenya: Waning Accountability for Justice*, 4; Oscar Mwangi, 'Corruption, Human Rights Violation and Counterterrorism Policies in Kenya', in *The Palgrave Handbook of Global Counterterrorism Policy*, ed. Scott Romaniuk, Francis Grice, Daniela Irrera and Stewart Webb (Basingstoke, Hampshire: Palgrave MacMillan, 2017), 1049–51.
29. Lind et al., 'Killing a Mosquito with a Hammer', 131.
30. AI, *Nowhere Else to Go*, 12.
31. Ibid., 12.
32. Ibid., 12.
33. Mark Bradbury and Michael Kleinman, *Winning Hearts and Minds? Examining the Relationship Between Aid and Security in Kenya* (Feinstein International Center, Tufts University, 2010), 21; UNHCR, 'Kenya: Figures at a Glance', http://www.unhcr.org; UNHCR, 'Dadaab Refugee Complex', http://www.unhcr.org.
34. AI, *Nowhere Else to Go*, 12–13.
35. Ibid., 12–13.
36. Lind et al., 'Killing a Mosquito with a Hammer', 131–2.
37. AI, *Nowhere Else to Go*, 13.
38. Thomson Reuters Foundation, *A Review of the Legal Framework*, 9.
39. Ibid., 9–10.

40. United Nations Security Council (UNSC), 'The Rule of Law and Transitional Justice in Conflict and Post-conflict Societies', *Report of the Secretary-General*, 23 August 2004, S/2004/616, 4.
41. Council of Europe (COE), *The Rule of Law Check List* (Venice: Council of Europe, 2016), 18–20.
42. Republic of Kenya, *The Constitution of Kenya* (Published by the National Council for Law Reporting with the Authority of the Attorney General, Revised Edition 2010), 13.
43. Ibid., 13.
44. Ibid., 14.
45. Ibid., 13.
46. Ibid., 70.
47. UNHCR, *1951 Convention Relating to the Status of Refugees*, 30.
48. Republic of Kenya, *Refugees Act No. 13 of 2006* (Published by the National Council for Law Reporting with the Authority of the Attorney-General, Revised Edition 2016 [2014]), 13.
49. UNHCR, *Somalia Situation: Supplementary Appeal* (Geneva: UNHCR, January–December 2017), 6.
50. AI, *Not Time to Go Home: Unsustainable Returns of Refugees to Somalia* (London: Amnesty International, 2017), 10.
51. Thomson Reuters Foundation, *A Review of the Legal Framework*, 10.
52. Ibid., 21–2.
53. AI, *Not Time to Go Home*, 21.
54. COE, *The Rule of Law*, 30–2.
55. Kenya, *The Constitution of Kenya*, 24.
56. Ibid., 19.
57. COE, *The Rule of Law*, 22.
58. UNHCR, *1951 Convention*, 30.
59. Kenya, *Refugees Act*, 13.
60. Ibid., 14.
61. Oscar Mwangi, 'The Dilemma of Kenya's New Counterterrorism and Asymmetric Warfare', *Peace Review: A Journal of Social Justice*, Special Issue on 'New' Conflicts and Emerging Economy of Difference in Africa 29, no. 3 (2017): 307–14, 311, doi:10.1080/10402659.2017.1344830.
62. Republic of Kenya, 'Closure of Dadaab to be Done within Confines of Law-AG', 8 June 2016, http://www.mygov.go.ke/closure-of-dadaab-to-be-done-within-confines-of-law-ag/; Republic of Kenya, 'Kenya's Decision to Close Dadaab Refugee Camp Final-DP Ruto', 23 May 2016, http://www.mygov.go.ke/kenyas-decision-to-close-dadaab-refugee-camp-final-dp-ruto/; Republic of Kenya, 'Government Update on the Repatriation of Refugees and Scheduled Closure of Dadaab Refugee Camp', 11 May 2016; Republic of Kenya, 'President Kenyatta's Madaraka Day Speech', 1 June 2016; Republic of Kenya, 'PS Karanja Kibicho Explains Why the Government is Shutting Down Refugee Camps', 9 May 2016; Republic of Kenya, 'Speech by His Excellency Hon. Uhuru Kenyatta, C.G.H., President of the Republic of Kenya and Commander in Chief of the Defence Forces, Extra-Ordinary Summit of the IGAD Assembly of Heads of State and Government on Durable Solutions for Somali Refugees', KICC, Nairobi, 25 March, 2017; National Police Service (NPS), 'Attack at Central Police Station - Mombasa', http://www.nationalpolice.go.ke/2015-09-08-17-56-33/news/173-attack-at-central-police-station-mombasa.html.
63. Ibid.
64. AI, *Somalis are Scapegoats in Kenya's Counter-Terror Crackdown* (London: Amnesty International, 2014), 5–6.
65. Independent Policing Oversight Authority (IPOA), *IPOA Report Following the Mpeketoni Attacks (15 and 16 June 2014) - Redacted Version* (Nairobi: IPOA, 2014), 3.
66. Ibid., 15.
67. IPOA, *IPOA Report*, 13–14; Mwangi, 'Corruption, Human Rights Violation', 1050.
68. Republic of Kenya, 'Gazette Notice No. 3017. The Refugees Act (No. 13 of 2006). Revocation of *Prima Facie* Refugee Status', *The Kenya Gazette* CXVIII, no. 46 (29 April 2016), 1901.

69. COE, *The Rule of Law*, 43–6.
70. Kenya, *The Constitution of Kenya*, 33–4.
71. Ibid., 96.
72. Republic of Kenya, Petition No. 19 of 2013 Consolidated with Petition No. 115 of 2013. Dated and delivered on 26 July 2013 (Nairobi: The National Council for Law Reporting, 2013), 1–5.
73. Ibid., 8–9.
74. Ibid., 24.
75. Republic of Kenya, Petition No. 628 of 2014 Consolidated with Petition No. 630 of 2014 and Petition No. 12 of 2015. Dated, Delivered and Signed on 23 February 2015 (Nairobi: The National Council for Law Reporting, 2015), 1–2.
76. Republic of Kenya, *The Security Laws (Amendment) Act, 2014 No. 19 of 2004. Kenya Gazette Supplement No. 167 (Acts No. 19)* (Nairobi: Government Printer, 2014), 341–2.
77. Kenya, Petition No. 628 of 2014 Consolidated with Petition No. 630 of 2014 and Petition No. 12 of 2015, 90–1.
78. Republic of Kenya, Constitutional Petition No. 227 of 2016. Dated, Delivered and Signed on 9 February 2017 (Nairobi: The National Council for Law Reporting, 2017), 2–3.
79. Ibid., 2–3.
80. Ibid., 12–15.
81. Victor Nyamori, *Kenya: Failure to Register Somali Refugees Putting Them at Risks of Starvation and Abuse* (Amnesty International, 20 February 2018), https://www.amnesty.org/en/latest/news/2018/02/kenya-failure-to-register-somali-refugees-putting-them-at-risk-of-starvation-and-abuse/.

Disclosure statement

No potential conflict of interest was reported by the author.

ORCID

Oscar Gakuo Mwangi http://orcid.org/0000-0002-3559-5900

The widespread use of torture in Mexico and its impacts on the rule of law

Denise González-Núñez

ABSTRACT

Torture is a widely diffused practice in Mexico, as has been reported for decades by civil society organisations, United Nations bodies and special procedures, and the National Human Rights Commission. Although torture has been used in various contexts, its use in criminal proceedings, as an 'illegal' method of criminal investigation to obtain confessions and incriminating statements, has been consistently denounced over the years. Encouraged by old court criteria, that translated into the lack of real judicial control, prosecutors have had no incentive to develop institutional capacities to investigate crimes on the basis of scientific evidence and excluding torture from their methods. Consequently, the possibility to develop institutional capacities to enforce the law according to human rights standards have been continuously undermined. With that in mind, the aim of this article is to analyse whether the systematic violation of the prohibition of torture (a *jus cogens* norm) by the Mexican State has had in impact on the rule of law, including in its substantive dimension, that is, the 'democratic rule of law'.

Introduction

There is no doubt that the prohibition of torture is a peremptory legal norm.[1] According to the International Court of Justice, it 'is part of customary international law and it has become a peremptory norm (*jus cogens*)'.[2] The peremptory character of this prohibition implies certain legal consequences and generates certain obligations on the States.[3]

However, the intention here is not to inquire as to said legal consequences and obligations, but rather to analyse whether the systematic violation of this *jus cogens* norm by a State may have an impact on the rule of law. The aim of this article is to address one of the questions raised by this special issue by giving a specific case example of 'in what ways the democratic rule of law within one or more democratic States is currently under siege through those States acquiescing to the erosion of customary and jus cogens legal norms domestically and/or internationally'. The example that will be used here is Mexico, a country where torture has been permanently denounced by civil society organisations and consistently reported by United Nations treaty bodies and special procedures to be widespread or systematic, especially in the context of criminal proceedings.

This article will be divided in two main sections. The first section analyses the continuity and systematicity of torture through qualitative and quantitative data from the sixties onwards. One must bear in mind though, that torture tends to be invisible or underreported, as many victims prefer not to complain out of fear of reprisals (in Mexico, as will be described below, those who are legally mandated to investigate torture are frequently the perpetrators). Consequently, several obstacles still prevent us from knowing the real magnitude of the problem. Additionally, although the available data allows us to observe certain patterns and trends, it is difficult to have the complete picture of its real evolution throughout the years.

The second section will analyse the impacts of the systematic violation of the prohibition of torture on the rule of law. For this purpose, and to understand the nature of State responsibility, a more detailed account of the specific circumstances in which torture has occurred over the years is given. Without pretending to carry out a very detailed legal analysis, this section aims to elucidate the nature of the Mexican authorities' responsibility. It is important insofar as it has had, as will be argued, a specific impact on the rule of law, which is addressed at the end of the section.

The main argument here is that the systematic violation of the prohibition of torture by Mexican authorities throughout the decades has eroded the rule of law in such a way that one of the State's most basic functions (and a core concept of the rule of law itself) -that is, the ability to enforce the law, specifically, to investigate and prosecute crimes-, has been seriously undermined. As will be argued, the systematic use of torture has eroded both the thin and thick concepts of the rule of law.[4]

I. The use of torture throughout the years: its continuous and systematic character

a). The use of torture as denounced by civil society organisations

Torture has been permanently denounced by civil society organisations in Mexico for at least six decades, although it may have received more attention in the context of certain social and political conflicts that have taken place. Reports date back to at least the period of the 'dirty war', which is referred to by some as a period of 'State terrorism'.[5] During the sixties and seventies, urban and rural *guerrilla* groups emerged demanding social changes.[6] Many of those who opposed the authoritarian regime of the Institutional Revolutionary Party (PRI for its acronym in Spanish), which governed the country from 1929 to the year 2000, were detained, tortured and disappeared or executed.[7]

Many organisations have denounced the violations that were committed,[8] but it is worth citing the report issued by the Special Prosecutor for Social and Political Movements of the Past, published in 2006 after national and international pressures were exerted on the federal government.[9] One section of said report addresses, for example, the use of torture in the case of 'El Quemado' (the name of a community in the state of Guerrero), clearly describes the *modus operandi* of federal agents:

> With them [the victims] a procedure was applied that later became recurrent to incriminate the transgressors and their supporters. Innocent people are incriminated, starting with

> breaking and entering, followed by search, pillage, forging of evidence, torture, a statement is made that incriminates the accused of crimes of which he is innocent, torture [is applied] so that he signs that statement, the accused is presented before the Prosecutor with the signed statement so that he presents him before the judge [...]. This procedure was followed at least in ninety documented cases of the people of El Quemado (own translation).[10]

This excerpt gives an account of the use of torture during that period of time, however, the reports of torture continued even after the 'dirty war'. In September 1991 Amnesty International published a report entitled 'Mexico: Torture and Impunity', after a country visit carried out in May and June 1990. Amnesty found that torture was widespread and that the victims were not circumscribed to a specific sector, but rather belonged to different groups, such as political activists, human rights defenders, union leaders, peasants, indigenous people and even children.[11] A follow-up report by the same organisation stated that 'it has received dozens of reports on maltreatment and torture inflicted by law enforcement officers'.[12]

A couple of years later after, there was another important period of social and political unrest framed in the process of implementing neoliberal economic policies in the country a process that reached its peak in January 1994 with the entry into force of the North American Free Trade Agreement. The armed uprising of the indigenous Zapatista National Liberation Army in the Southern state of Chiapas that same year and a serious economic crisis that started in December 1994 were both part of an otherwise politically agitated country.

In reaction to the indigenous uprising the federal government deployed the military in the region, especially in those communities where the Zapatistas had influence and presence.[13] By 1998 the military was present in 66 municipalities in Chiapas.[14] The victims of human rights violations were mainly peasants and political activists[15] who were interrogated 'about the whereabouts of weapons and who the Zapatistas were'.[16]

In that context, torture was again documented, along with arbitrary detention, enforced disappearance, among others,[17] and continued to be reported by organisations for the next decades, even in the absence of social conflicts as those mentioned above. In fact, in the year 2003 -three years after the PRI candidate was finally defeated in elections – Amnesty International published a report stating that

> [d]uring the last thirty years, [it] has reported on the widespread and systematic use torture in Mexico [and] continues to receive persistent reports on torture every year; what is more, it is evident that torture continues to be an endemic practice at the state and municipal level.[18]

Only a few days after president Felipe Calderon took power in 1 December 2006, a new drug policy was implemented. The armed forces and the federal police were deployed in the streets of the state of Michoacán to supposedly restore 'peace in every region that is threatened by organized crime'.[19] Soon after, military-led operations were extended to northern states like Baja California, Sinaloa and Chihuahua and eventually to the rest of the country reaching 50,000 soldiers by 2012.[20] Their activities have included patrolling, establishing checkpoints, seising drugs, money and weapons, eradicating crops and arresting alleged drug-lords and organised criminals.[21]

The social toll of this new policy proved to be immense over the years. When the United Nations High Commissioner for Human Rights visited Mexico in October 2015, he expressed his concern by underlining that

> [f]or a country that is not engaged in a conflict, the estimated figures are simply staggering: 151,233 people killed between December 2006 and August 2015, including thousands of transiting migrants. At least 26,000 people missing, many believed to be as a result of enforced disappearances, since 2007 [...].[22]

Torture has been among the many human rights violations that have been denounced by civil organisations in the context of the aforementioned policy. Amnesty International even entitled a 2014 report as 'Out of Control: Torture and other ill-treatment in Mexico', which found *again* that there was a 'widespread' use of torture.[23] Other reports by the same organisation followed, all of which highlighted the 'epidemic' of torture and the impunity that followed.[24] Amnesty's findings add up to multiple reports published by several international and local human rights organisations to denounce the use of torture and ill-treatment committed by public security-related officers, including police and armed forces.[25]

b). The use of torture as reported by United Nations treaty bodies and special procedures

In December 2014 the United Nations (UN) Special Rapporteur on torture and other cruel, inhuman or degrading treatment or punishment, Mr. Juan E. Méndez, published his report on Mexico after a country visit carried out in March–April of the same year. After analyzing extensive information received before and during his visit, the report reached strong conclusions that started off with the statement that '[t]orture and ill-treatment in the moments following detention and before detainees are brought before a judge **are generalised in Mexico and occur in a context of impunity**' (emphasis added).[26]

Strongly opposed by the Mexican government, the report was considered to be a confirmation of what appeared to be evident in the eyes of civil society organisations and victims' groups: Mexico was (and arguably *is*) going through a human rights crisis,[27] of which torture is just one of its expressions. To illustrate the gravity of the situation, in his report the Rapporteur mentioned that between 2006 and April 2014, a total of 11,608 complaints of torture and ill-treatment were received by Mexico's National Human Rights Commission.[28] The follow-up report presented in 2017 by the next Special Rapporteur on Torture, Nils Melzer, concluded that 'torture and mistreatment continue to be widespread in Mexico' (own translation).[29]

It is important to mention that these reports were not the first UN reports to point out the magnitude and/or recurrence of the problem of torture in Mexico. On the contrary, UN bodies have expressed concern regarding the latter almost as early as their first reports on Mexico. In 1993, the UN Committee against Torture issued its Concluding Observations on the second period report of Mexico and 'expressed concern at the reports they had received from non-governmental organizations which appeared to point to the **continued** practice of torture'.[30] In similar terms, in 1998 the then Special Rapporteur on Torture, Sir Nigel S. Rodley, visited Mexico for the first time and, in his report, noted 'the great deal of information from non-governmental sources to the effect that torture **continued** to be a **common** practice' (emphasis added).[31]

Between the years 2000 and 2010, at least ten reports produced by different UN bodies (both treaty bodies and special procedures) expressed their concern regarding said human rights violation.[32] The UN Committee against Torture's 2003 report on Mexico, from which the following lines are extracted, is outstanding in underlining the systematic use of torture in similar terms to those used by the Rapporteur 14 years later:

> [T]he information collected in the course of this procedure [...] convinced the Committee members that **these are not exceptional situations or occasional violations** committed by a few police officers but that, on the contrary, the police **commonly use torture and resort to it systematically** [...] (emphasis added).[33]

Considering that torture is usually a concealed practice with some form of official participation, it is difficult to register the real magnitude of the problem, or at least it has been in the case of Mexico. A number of obstacles in this regard were mentioned by the Rapporteur back in 2014, namely, the lack of a national register of cases, the fact that each state keeps its own data, an unknown number of unreported cases due to fear of reprisals and an official practice of classifying torture as ill-treatment or other less serious crime (e.g. abuse of authority).[34] However, the international bodies' observations regarding the situation of torture in Mexico have shown the persistence of this human rights violation throughout the years.

The seriousness of the problem has been even acknowledged by regional bodies such as the Inter-American Commission of Human Rights, who corroborated in 2015 that 'the prevalence of the practice of torture is also alarming in Mexico'.[35] In its report the Commission added that it had 'received information indicating that official records on torture and ill-treatment across the country are under-inclusive and are inaccurate, contradictory, and incomplete, which makes it impossible to get an accurate picture of the real magnitude of the problem'.[36]

c). The use of torture as reported by the National Human Rights Commission

Another available source of information regarding torture in Mexico are the annual reports of the National Human Rights Commission ('the National Commission' or NHRC).[37] The National Commission's statics are limited due to several reasons.[38] However, they allow us to observe the overall trends that the filing of complaints for torture or CIDT have had since 1990.

From 1990 to the year 2000 the NHRC changed seven times the temporality covered by each annual report, which makes it difficult to compare the data. From 2001 onwards it has kept to a January-December format. To facilitate the analysis two tables are presented below with data related to torture and/or CIDT complaints registered in two large periods of time: 1990–2000 (Table 1) and 2001–2017 (Table 2).

The number of complaints increased between 1992 and 1997, which coincides with -and may be attributed to- the human rights violations committed in the context of the Zapatista conflict. Torture complaints specifically report two peaks: one in 1991 and another in 1992–1994 and an apparent decrease afterwards. However, one must bear in mind that the 1992 constitutional decree that transformed NHRC into an autonomous body established a one-year period of time for the local commissions to be created.[39] The decrease that can be observed from 1993 onwards may be explained by said 'decentralization'.[40]

In fact, according to a 1995 human rights report published by the Miguel Agustin Pro Human Rights Center:

Table 1. Torture complaints annually registered by the NHRC, 1990–2000.

Period of time	Total number of complaints registered by the NHRC (different human rights violations)	Total number of torture complaints	% represented by torture complaints from the total number of complaints registered by the NRHC
June–Decemeber 1990	1343	150	11.1
Decemeber 1990–June 1991	1913	225	11.7
June–December 1991	2485	119	4.7
December 1991–May 1992	4503	52	1.2
May 1992–May 1993	8793	113	1.2
May 1993–May 1994	8804	79	0.8
May 1994–May 1995	8912	31	0.3
May 1995–May 1996	8357	40	0.4
May 1996–May 1997	8509	35	0.4
May–Decemeber 1997	5943	39	0.6
Jan–December 1998	6523	21	0.3
Jan–November 1999	5402	6	0.1
November 1999–November 2000	4473	9	0.2

Source: Taken from the NHRC annual reports.

Table 2. Torture complaints annually registered by the NHRC, 2001–2017.

Year	Total number of complaints registered by the NHRC	Number of complaints in which CIDT was allegedly committed against the complainant	Number of complaints in which torture was allegedly committed against the complainant	Number of complaints in which torture or CIDT were allegedly committed against the complainant	% represented by torture complaints from the total number of complaints registered by the NHRC	% represented by torture and CIDT complaints from the total number of complaints registered by the NHRC
2001	4195	208	9	217	0.21454	5.17282
2002	3918	177	19	196	0.48494	5.00255
2003	4071	206	13	219	0.31933	5.37951
2004	4643	268	5	273	0.10769	5.87982
2005	6137	271	2	273	0.03259	4.44843
2006	6895	330	6	336	0.08702	4.8731
2007	6535	395	4	399	0.06121	6.10559
2008	7546	987	21	1008	0.27829	13.3581
2009	7703	1105	33	1138	0.4284	14.7735
2010	8593	1170	10	1180	0.11637	13.7321
2011	12601	1626	42	1668	0.33331	13.237
2012	14865	1642	20	1662	0.13454	11.1806
2013	13636	1078	4	1082	0.02933	7.93488
2014	12285	741	3	744	0.02442	6.05617
2015	15243	663	50	713	0.32802	4.67756
2016	14494	528	216	744	1.49027	5.13316
2017	14156	319	83	402	0.58632	2.83979

Source: Made with data recovered from NHRC annual reports and calculations of my own.

> [c]ontrary to what was stated by the CNDH, the number of victims of torture does not seem to decrease substantially in relation to previous years. Less complaints are probably being filed before the national *ombudsman* since it was decentralized to local bodies, but the number of human rights violations due to torture continues to be a cause for concern (own translation).[41]

According to this organisation's historical records, the total number of 'violations' for torture reached 142 in 1995.[42]

The number of complaints filed for torture recorded in Table 2 may be relatively low compared to the total number of complaints registered by the Commission each year. But adding those to the number of complaints filed for CIDT renders a higher percentage from the total number of complaints registered annually. It can be observed that the number of complaints both for CIDT and torture have an important increase in two years: 2008 and 2011. This change coincides with the implementation of the drug-related policy mentioned earlier and the following increase in human rights violations as denounced by civil society organisations.[43]

In the year 2007, 6.1% of the complaints filed before the NHRC involved torture or ill-treatment. In 2008 it was 13.3%, which represents an increase rate of 152% in the number of complaints filed for torture and CIDT with respect to 2007. In the year 2011 there was another steep increase both in the number of complaints filed before the National Commission and the number of those where torture and ill-treatment were allegedly committed. Particularly the latter increased at a rate of 318% with respect to 2007.

In sum, even if documenting torture and CIDT can be difficult and without pretending to make any statistical inferences, it can be argued that there is sufficient data to support the conclusion that torture has indeed been a widely diffused and prevalent practice in Mexico for at least six decades, although Mexican authorities have consistently denied it arguing that it is limited to some 'isolated cases'.[44]

II. The impacts of the systematic violation of the prohibition of torture on the rule of law

a). State responsibility in the systematic violation of the prohibition of torture and the consequent erosion of the ability to investigate and prosecute

In spite of important normative developments[45] and the fact the prohibition of torture is a *jus cogens* norm, human rights organisations and the UN Rapporteurs themselves have been able to document the use of torture in several contexts, such as social protests and others.[46] However, it has been prominently committed while detainees are under the custody of the security forces (whether civil or military) or the prosecutor's office. In other words, it has been very commonly committed in the context of criminal proceedings.

In 1991 Amnesty International reported that usually when the police felt pressured to solve a specific case they apprehended political activists or criminal suspects or even randomly selected people in the street, forced them to confess through torture and incommunicado detention and presented said confessions in the courts, who 'frequently admit as evidence confessions obtained under torture rendered by those criminally accused, although it is strictly prohibited in national and international legislation'.[47] It furthermore stated that torture mainly happened in the context of criminal investigations and that in fact, according to the cases brought to their attention, coerced confessions were many times the sole evidence used by the courts to convict those accused.[48]

In 1997 the UN Special Rapporteur on Torture, Sir Nigel Rodley, pointed out that torture and CIDT had been generally committed 'in the course of crime investigations'.[49] According to the UN CAT Committee (2003),

> [i]n most cases torture is resorted to as a means of obtaining information quickly and easily for later use in criminal proceedings ... Those chiefly responsible are members of judicial police forces (*policias judiciales*, called *policias ministeriales* in some States) at both State and Federal level.[50]

In 2014, the then UN Special Rapporteur, Mr. Juan Méndez, came to the similar conclusions: '[t]orture is used mainly from the moment when a person is detained until he is brought before the judicial authority'.[51]

The latter seems to be corroborated with the recurrence with which certain state agencies are accused of torture. Each year the NHRC has identified a diversity of state agencies to be allegedly responsible for the acts of torture brought to its attention via the non-jurisdictional complaint mechanism (i.e. not considering CIDT complaints) including local and federal police, local prosecutors, immigration enforcement personnel, among others.[52] Not surprisingly, the great majority of the state agencies identified annually as being allegedly responsible for torture belong either to the civil law enforcement *corps* or the military.

Between 2001 and 2014, the General Prosecutor's Office and the Secretary of National Defense were identified to be allegedly responsible for committing torture almost every year.[53] In the case of said Secretary, the number of times it was pointed out as the alleged responsible agency in the complaints seriously increased between 2008 and 2012, which coincides with the launching of the 'war on drugs' and the militarisation of public safety, as mentioned earlier.

As for the purpose of torture, human rights organisations have consistently denounced that torture has been committed to coerce confessions, which have historically been one of the pillars on which has rested the prosecutors' criminal proceedings and conviction,[54] or to cover other human rights violations, such as arbitrary detention. The UN Committee against Torture gave voice to these concerns as early as 1993, on the occasion of the second periodic report of Mexico. In its Concluding Observations, the Committee stated 'it also appeared that confessions occupied an important place in the system of evidence and that the police felt obliged to obtain confessions even through means of torture'.[55] The Committee added that 'State officials prosecuted for having practiced torture themselves complained that they were forced to confess under torture'.[56]

The Committee's 2003 report cited earlier added that torture was *systematically* used in Mexico '**as another method of criminal investigation**, readily available whenever required in order to advance the process'.[57] Additionally, in 2012 the same Committee expressed that it was

> gravely concerned by consistent reports that, before detainees are handed over to the Prosecution Service, they are tortured and mistreated in order to force them to confess and make self-incriminating statements which are later used to cover up irregularities committed during their detention.[58]

Finally, the Special Rapporteur's 2014 report observed, among other things, 'disturbing similarities among testimonies' relating to the methods and the objectives of torture, namely 'to punish and to extract confessions or incriminating information'.[59] According to the Miguel Agustin Pro Human Rights Center, 'a very important number of registered cases fit in the pattern of arbitrary detention-torture-fabrication of illegal evidence-criminal process' (own translation).[60]

More recently, organisations have denounced that confessions are obtained through torture in substitution of scientifically-based criminal investigations.[61] In other words, instead of carrying out criminal investigations on the basis of scientific and forensic expertise oriented by a theory of each case, police and prosecutors have used and relied on torture as an 'illegal' method to obtain confessions and thus to bring cases before the courts.[62] In fact, according to a 2012 study published by a nationally recognised academic institution, cited by the Rapporteur in his 2014 report, '57.2% of detainees in federal centres said that they had been beaten during their detention and 34.6% said that they had been forced to sign or alter a confession'.[63]

The use of torture to obtain confessions can find its source in the Mexican criminal justice system, with its formerly inquisitorial character, and with principles and judicial interpretations that were contrary to the presumption of innocence and other due process standards.[64] One of said principles is that of 'procedural immediacy'. According to the judicial interpretation given to this principle, 'the first declarations of the accused prevail over the subsequent ones' arguably given that they were rendered spontaneously, closer in time to the commission of the crime and before the accused has been 'taught' by his defense attorney on what to say before the judge.[65] This principle has been applied in criminal cases to discard exculpatory statements made by the accused before the judge taking back a confession made before the prosecutor.[66] It has been applied even to discard statements where the victims of a crime have taken back a prior one where they identified the accused as the alleged responsible.[67]

In addition to the aforementioned principle, the judicial interpretation of the law regarding the confession's value as evidence in criminal proceedings has had also a perverse effect in prosecutorial practices. According to old court criteria, 'the confession of the defendant that has not been dismissed and has been strengthened with other means of conviction in the case, produces full evidence and is sufficient to substantiate a conviction'.[68] Although the decision from which this judicial criterion was taken dates from 1989, it can be traced even to the fifties.[69] Hence, the Mexican criminal system has given a vital role to the first statements rendered by the accused and to their confessions creating the right incentives for police and prosecutors to obtain confessions even if it is through torture. In this system, judges did not exercise real control on detentions carried out by the police and the rendering of declarations before the prosecutor.

Fortunately, a series of legal reforms have taken place. Article 20 of the Federal Constitution of Mexico was reformed in 2008 to allow the criminal justice system to transit from an inquisitorial system to an adversarial one. Section A, fraction IX of said reformed article states that '[a]ny evidence obtained in violation of fundamental rights will be null'. Additionally, the first judgements issued by the Inter-American Court of Human Rights against Mexico in 2009 triggered a series of discussions at the National Supreme Court of Justice related to the Judicial Branch's international obligations.[70] Moreover, the 2011 constitutional reform established a new paradigm around human rights, State duties and rules of interpretation. In 2014, a new National Code of Criminal Procedure came into force.

Furthermore, renewed judicial interpretation has been elaborated around the principle of 'procedural immediacy'. According to a May 2017 federal court decision, the principle of procedural immediacy lacks any value 'if the accused issued the statement in question in order to negotiate the possibility that his torment would cease'.[71] Finally, in June 2017 Congress passed the General Law to Prevent, Investigate and Sanction *Torture* and Other Cruel, Inhuman and Degrading Treatment, with an entire chapter of rules for the exclusion of illegal evidence.

However, it is probably easier to change the law (without underestimating decades of important work done by human rights organisations, scholars and congress people themselves), than to remove old practices from institutions that have operated for decades under certain rules. The case of the enforced disappearance of 43 students from the Rural Teacher's College in Ayotzinapa, state of Guerrero, in September 2014 serves as a tragic example.

In 2016 this paradigmatic case of enforced disappearance in Mexico was confirmed to be also a paradigmatic case of torture when the Interdisciplinary Group of Independent Experts ('Group of Experts') of the Inter-American Commission on Human Rights published its second report on the case. In said report the Group concluded, among other things, that the available evidence showed 'significant signs of ill-treatment and torture'.[72] The 17 people that were arrested for the enforced disappearance of the 43 students presented new injuries after being detained and at least 5 of them confessed that the students' bodies were burned in a dumpsite in Cocula, state of Guerrero, a theory of the case that was presented as the 'historical truth' of the destiny of the students by the Federal Prosecutor's Office in a press conference in January 2015. This theory was discarded one month later through an expert report issued by the *Argentine Forensic Anthropology Team* (EAAF) stating that it 'does not support the hypothesis that there was a fire of the required magnitude and the duration reported in the early morning hours of September 27 that would have resulted in mass incineration of the 43 disappeared students' (own translation).[73]

This case is paradigmatic of torture because, notwithstanding the fact that it was a cause for national and international scandal,[74] that international human rights bodies were paying close attention to the authorities' performance and that new criminal rules were already in place, the Federal Prosecutor's Office was apparently not able to build a criminal case on the basis of objective evidence and exclude torture or any kind of ill-treatment as a method of investigation. In fact, the Group of Experts concluded in their second report the following:

> The relevance of the confessions and the statements of the accused as evidence in criminal investigations in Mexico is huge. It seems that the queen of evidence to advance an investigation is the statement and that the decisive evidence to impute responsibilities is the confession. Objective and scientific evidence is secondary and, in many cases, even exceptional for this purpose.[75]

After decades of international scrutiny and important legislative reform, the Group of Experts came to conclusions that were very similar in terms to that of the UN Committee against Torture in 1993 regarding the use of torture by public officers and the role played by confessions in criminal proceedings. In summary, the data allows us to conclude that torture has been and continues to be directly committed by state agents, namely police officers, prosecutors and the military, as an 'illegal' method of criminal investigation that ends up almost entirely substituting other prosecutorial efforts, such as the collection of scientific evidence.

b). Impacts on the rule of law

The concept of the rule of law has been widely discussed in the literature.[76] According to Tomuschat, '[i]t is a perennial theme of constitutional philosophy'.[77] Authors have agreed that there is no one definition of rule of law, but rather several definitions that elaborate the concept either from a thin and formal perspective or from a thick and substantive one.[78]

Peerenboom explains that the rule of law, in its thin version, is basically understood as a system of laws that are 'general, public, prospective, clear, consistent, capable of being followed, stable, impartially applied and enforced … [and] reasonably acceptable to a majority of the populace … '.[79] This is what Fox-Decent calls the 'no-rights thesis', which is based on the idea that the law exists to guide behaviour and that 'the rule of law goes to the manner in which laws are formulated and enforced rather than the substantive content of particular laws'.[80]

In line with this, the World Justice Project, which created the Rule of Law Index, builds its indicators on the basis of two main principles. First, 'whether the law imposes limits on the exercise of power by the state and its agents'. Second,

> whether the state limits the actions of members of society and fulfills its basic duties towards its population so that the public interest is served, people are protected from violence, and all members of society have access to dispute settlement and grievance mechanisms.[81]

The concept of 'liberal democratic rule of law' is a thick version of the concept, which builds on the formal one by adding some elements, such as 'free market capitalism […], multiparty democracy in which citizens choose their representatives at all levels of government and a liberal interpretation of human rights […]'.[82] The definition of rule of law included in the UN Secretary General 2004 report embraces the substantive concept by including equality before the law, accountability, participation in the decision-making process, legal transparency, among other elements.[83]

In my analysis, the widely diffused practice of torture in criminal proceedings in Mexico, as exposed earlier, has had an impact in the rule of law, both in its substantive and formal dimensions. In relation to the former, the practice of torture (encouraged by certain legal criteria) has reinforced practices that are inconsistent with human rights, even in the presence of international obligations mandating otherwise. In this sense, the practice of torture has been one of the fundamental parts of a vicious circle that has consistently eroded the democratic rule of law.

Furthermore, the systematic violation of the prohibition of torture has had an impact in the rule of law in its formal dimension. The widely diffused practice of torture has continuously undermined state capacity to investigate crimes by limiting prosecutorial activity to the extraction of confessions and consequently inhibiting the development of scientifically-based criminal investigation techniques. The State has thus lost its capacity to enforce the law, which is one of the basic ideas around which the concept of *thin* rule of law is constructed, rendering the notion of 'accountability to the laws' to a mere discourse founded on State simulation.

On 5 September 2018 important information was published in the Mexican digital media platform '*Animal Político*'. The title read as follows: 'In 2018 judges have dismissed 80% of the cases brought by the PGR [General Prosecutor of the Republic, here referred to as the Federal Prosecutor's Office]; six times more than at the beginning of the administration' (own translation).[84] The piece explained that the PGR had allegedly become more ineffective when building the criminal cases and supported this explanation with data: while in 2013 the percentage of dismissal was 12.9%, in 2018 it reached 80.2%.[85]

However, I believe that there is another explanation for the increase of dismissed cases. That is, not that the PGR has become more ineffective in the last five years (as it has always been), but that courts are now starting to exercise *real* judicial control. If my theory is correct, then courts should be imposing new and higher standards for prosecutors.[86] The problem is, that after decades of not exercising said control and having incorrect incentives operating in the criminal justice system (those that promoted torture instead of discouraging it) Mexico has been left with both a prosecutorial culture and a set of practices that lack the tools and expertise necessary to carry out professional investigations, that is, based on scientific evidence and beyond extracting confessions through torture.

The above has translated into an almost absolute incapacity to enforce the law. With an 80.2% of dismissed criminal cases, I believe that it can be safely said that the rule of law, even in its thin version, has been seriously eroded. Without a Federal Prosecutor's Office that is capable of carrying out its mandate according to certain standards and norms (such as the absolute prohibition of torture), the task of investigating crimes seems to be an unsurmountable challenge. This puts the State's basic duty of enforcing its system of laws entirely at risk, or at least in relation to one of two main State actors in charge of said duty: the prosecutor. Suddenly, the possibility of holding accountable those responsible for committing crimes (an element of the thin definition of rule of law) is at stake and, at the same time, doing so in full respect of the human dignity (which is part of the thick definition of rule of law). Not surprisingly, Mexico is among the countries with weakest rule of law worldwide, ranking 92 out of 113 in the Rule of Law Index 2017–2018.[87]

The piece published recently by *Animal Politico* gives additional information that supports the latter: in the last eight years the Federal Prosecutor's Office has opened (or attracted from state jurisdiction) more than 400 investigations for homicide, but has obtained only two convictions.[88] In my analysis, this information is a sign of the lack of capacities to investigate a 'standard' crime such as homicide and thus an indication of State incapacity to protect the population and ensure its safety, which is the State's basic function. Now imagine the collapse of the Mexican prosecutorial institutions *vis-à-vis* the investigation of more complex crimes such as enforced disappearance, which according to the UN Committee on Enforced Disappearances is 'widespread' in much of the Mexican territory.[89] As was referred to earlier, prosecutors appear to be so dependent on the use of torture, that not even in the paradigmatic case of Ayotzinapa was the Federal Prosecutor's Office able to resort to a different set of practices.

In June 2018 a federal appeals court analyzing the merits of a writ of *amparo* promoted by the accused in the Ayotzinapa case concluded, among other things, that there were sufficient grounds to presume that confessions were obtained through torture; that self-incriminating declarations had a limited probative effectiveness; that the investigation of the forcefully disappeared students 'was not prompt, effective, independent or impartial'; and that 'in the light of Inter-American Jurisprudence, this situation must be remedied'.[90] Therefore, *acknowledging the inefficacy* of the Federal Prosecutor's Office to investigate, the appeals court ordered the trial court to reinstate the procedure against the defendants with a series of guarantees, such as the carrying out of the Istanbul Protocol.[91] Furthermore, the appeals court ordered an alternative measure to access truth and justice: the creation of a special Inquiry Commission.[92]

Conclusions

The available qualitative and quantitative data indicates that torture is a widely diffused practice in Mexico in criminal investigations. Both national and international human rights organisations have denounced the use of torture in Mexico at least since the 'dirty war', during the sixties and seventies. United Nations treaty bodies and special procedures have consistently reported, at least since 1993, that torture is 'common', 'widespread' or otherwise 'systematic'. Although limited, the statistics kept by the National Human Rights Commission show the continuity of torture and ill-treatment complaints and their overall trends since 1990. Without seeking to prove a statistical correlation, these trends coincide with certain periods of social unrest in Mexico, although -as has been said- torture has been permanently denounced by civil society.

In committing torture, state agents have had a direct responsibility. Law-enforcement officers, namely police and prosecutors, and the military have been frequently identified as the perpetrators. Although torture has been used in various contexts, its use in criminal proceedings has been consistently reported over the years. In that context, torture has been a prosecutorial tool to obtain confessions or incriminating statements from detainees. In this sense, torture has been used as an 'illegal' method of criminal investigation, encouraged by old court criteria that gave confessions a preponderant value in the proceedings. In spite of constitutional and legislative reforms, and the ratification of almost every human rights treaty, prosecutors in Mexico have continued to rely strongly on confessions and incriminating statements when allegedly carrying out their mandate.

Without adequate judicial control, prosecutors have had no incentive to develop institutional capacities to investigate crimes on the basis of scientific evidence and excluding torture from their methods. This has translated in an almost absolute incapacity to enforce the law according to human rights standards. The systematic violation of the prohibition of torture, hence the systematic violation of this *jus cogens* norm, has therefore undermined the rule of law both in its 'substantive' and 'formal' dimensions.

In relation to the former, the use of torture has reinforced practices that violate human dignity and are inconsistent with human rights. As regards the latter, torture has continuously undermined state capacity to investigate crimes by limiting prosecutorial activity to the extraction of confessions and consequently inhibiting the development of scientifically-based criminal investigation techniques. In other words, by committing or acquiescing to torture, prosecutors have self-sabotaged their own prosecutorial mandate. With the lack of said institutional capacities, the possibility of holding accountable those responsible for committing crimes and thus protecting the population seems an unsurmountable challenge to Mexican prosecutors.

Consequently, it is possible to say not only that the 'democratic rule of law' has been adversely affected in Mexico, but even that the most basic concept of 'rule of law' has been eroded. This explanation may be over simplistic and is assuredly lacking of a more profound analysis on the responsibilities of prosecutors in the commission of torture and the reasons behind the underdevelopment of their institutional capacities (or even a sociological analysis of the organisational culture of criminal justice personnel), but it may offer some light as to how the democratic rule of law within a State can be undermined through the violation of *jus cogens* legal norms, such as the absolute prohibition of torture.

Notes

1. Daniel Costelloe, *Legal Consequences of Peremptory Norms in International Law* (Cambridge: Cambridge University Press, 2017) Kindle Edition, 16.
2. Ibid., 51.
3. Erika de Wet, 'The Prohibition of Torture as an International Norm of *jus cogens* and its Implications for National and Customary Law', *European Journal of International Law* 15, no. 1 (2004): 97–100.
4. Randall Peerenboom, 'Human Rights and Rule of Law: What's the relationship?', *Research Paper no. 05–31,* Public Law & Legal Theory Research Paper Series (Los Angeles: University of California School of Law, 2005); Christian Tomuschat, 'Democracy and the Rule of Law', in *International Human Rights Law,* ed. Dinah Shelton (Oxford: Oxford University Press, 2013), Kindle Edition.
5. Andrea Radilla Martínez and Claudia E.G. Rangel Lozano, coords., *Desaparición Forzada y Terrorismo de Estado en México* (Madrid: Plaza y Valdés Editores, 2012).
6. Laura Castellanos, *México Armado 1943–1981* (Mexico City: Biblioteca Era, 2008).
7. Luis Arriaga Valenzuela, 'Crímenes de Estado y Derechos Humanos en México', *El Cotidiano* 23, no. 150 (2008): 58.
8. Centro de Derechos Humanos Miguel Agustín Pro Juárez et al., *Desapariciones Forzadas durante la Guerra Sucia en México e Impunidad* (31 Mayo 2014), https://tbinternet.ohchr.org/Treaties/CED/Shared%20Documents/MEX/INT_CED_ICO_MEX_17810_S.pdf; Hilda Navarrete Gorjón et al., *Informe Final de Actividades* (Comisión de la Verdad del Estado de Guerrero, October 15, 2014); Radilla and Rangel, *Desaparición Forzada.*
9. Office of Special Prosecutor Ignacio Carrillo Prieto, *Historical Report to the Mexican Society* (2006), https://nsarchive2.gwu.edu/NSAEBB/NSAEBB209/index.htm#informe; Alfredo Méndez Ortiz, 'La Femospp se extingue sin conseguir que se castigue a presuntos represores', *La Jornada,* March 27, 2007, http://www.jornada.com.mx/2007/03/27/index.php?section=politica&article=014n1pol. The office of the Special Prosecutor was opened in 2002 after the 2000 election, when the PRI was defeated. However, it was closed in 2007 with not even one judgment issued for human rights violations committed during.
10. Office of the Special Prosecutor Ignacio Carrillo Prieto, *Historical Report,* 543.
11. Amnesty International, *México: Tortura e Impunidad* (Madrid: Editorial Amnistía Internacional, 1991) AMR 41/O3/91/s, 7.
12. Amnesty International, *Recent Developments Relevant to the Issue of Torture* (September 1991) AMR 41/10/91/s, https://www.amnesty.org/download/Documents/196000/amr410101991es.pdf.
13. Centro de Derechos Humanos Fray Bartolomé de las Casas, *La Legalidad de la Injusticia* (San Cristóbal de las Casas: Centro de Derechos Humanos Fray Bartolomé de las Casas, 1998), https://frayba.org.mx/historico/archivo/informes/980801_la_legalidad_de_la_injusticia_frayba.pdf, 51.

14. Ibid., 51.
15. Carmen Pedrazzini, 'La represión del Estado', in *Los Derechos Humanos en México durante la Transición Sexenal,* coord. David Fernández (Mexico City: Universidad Iberoamericana Ciudad de México & Centro de Derechos Humanos Miguel Agustín Pro Juárez, 1995), 19; Centro de Derechos Humanos Fray Bartolomé de las Casas, *Let's raise our voices for justice!* (San Cristóbal de las Casas: Centro de Derechos Humanos Fray Bartolomé de las Casas, 1996), https://frayba.org.mx/wp-content/uploads/2017/02/960220_lets_raise_our_voices_for_justice_frayba.pdf, 23. Several other reports by this organisation can be accessed in https://frayba.org.mx/historico/informes.php?page=10&hl=es&tag_ID=19.
16. Centro de Derechos Humanos Fray Bartolomé de las Casas, *Let's raise our voices for justice!*, 23.
17. Pedrazzini, 'La represión del Estado', 19.
18. Amnesty International, *Mexico. Unfair Trials: Unsafe Convictions* (March 2003) AMR 41/007/2003, https://www.amnesty.org/download/Documents/104000/amr410072003es.pdf.
19. Claudia Herrera and Ernesto Martínez, 'Vestido Militar, Calderón rinde "Tributo" a las Fuerzas Armadas', *La Jornada,* January 4, 2001, http://www.jornada.unam.mx/2007/01/04/index.php?section=politica&article=003n1pol; Francisco Relea, 'Entrevista a Felipe Calderón: La situación en México', *El País,* January 21, 2007, http://www.elpais.com/articulo/internacional/Mexico/corria/riesgo/ser/dominado/crimen/elpepiint/20070121elpepiint_5/Tes?print=1.
20. Human Rights Council, *Report of the Special Rapporteur on Torture and other Cruel, Inhuman or Degrading Treatment or Punishment, Juan E. Méndez. Addendum. Mission to Mexico* (December 29, 2014), U.N.Doc. A/HRC/28/68/Add.3 par. 20.
21. Marcos Muedano, 'Disminuye 67% la quema de yerba', *Excelsior,* July 29, 2018, https://www.excelsior.com.mx/nacional/disminuye-67-la-quema-de-yerba/1255293; Marcos Muedano, 'Destruyen más de 26 mil armas decomisadas al crimen organizado', *Excelsior,* October 25, 2018, https://www.excelsior.com.mx/nacional/destruyen-mas-de-26-mil-armas-decomisadas-al-crimen-organizado/1274203; Michelle Mejía, 'La batalla del Ejército contra las drogas en el "Triángulo Dorado"', *Uno TV,* April 22, 2017, https://www.unotv.com/noticias/portal/nacional/detalle/la-batalla-del-ejrcito-contra-las-drogas-en-el-tringulo-dorado-820024/;
Manu Ureste, 'Un recorrido por los corruptos retenes retenes del ejército de México', *Insight crime,* January 15, 2015, https://es.insightcrime.org/noticias/analisis/recorrido-corruptos-retenes-ejercito-mexico/; The heads of public security agencies were also gradually substituted by the military. Marcelo Galán, 'Militares a cargo de la seguridad en 17 entidades', *El Universal,* February 28, 2011, http://archivo.eluniversal.com.mx/primera/36411.html.
22. Zeid Ra'ad Al Hussein, 'Statement of the UN High Commissioner for Human Rights' (Mexico City, October 7, 2015), https://www.ohchr.org/en/NewsEvents/Pages/DisplayNews.aspx?NewsID=16578.
23. Amnesty International, *Out of Control: Torture and Other Ill-Treatment in Mexico* (London: Amnesty International, 2014), AMR 41/020/2014.
24. Amnesty International, *Paper Promises, Daily Impunity: Mexicós Torture Epidemic Continues* (London: Amnesty International, 2015) AMR 41/2676/2015; *Surviving Death: Police and Military Torture of Women in Mexico* (London: Amnesty International, 2016), AMR 41/4237/2016.
25. *See*, for example, Human Rights Watch, *Neither Rights Nor Security. Killings, Torture, and Disappearances in Mexico's 'War on Drugs'* (United States of America: Human Rights Watch, 2011), https://www.hrw.org/sites/default/files/reports/mexico1111webwcover_0.pdf; ACAT-France, *Au nom de la 'guerre contre le crime'. Une étude du phénomene tortionnaire au Mexique* (ACAT-France, 2012), https://www.acatfrance.fr/rapport/au-nom-de-la-guerre-contre-le-crime; Centro de Derechos Humanos Miguel Agustín Pro Juárez, *La Magnitud de la Crisis de Derechos Humanos en México en el Marco de las Políticas de Seguridad Pública y del Sistema de Justicia Penal* (Mexico City: Centro de Derechos Humanos Miguel Agustín Pro Juárez, 2016), http://centroprodh.org.mx/index.php?option=com_docman&task=doc_details&gid=214&Itemid=28&lang=es; Ximena Suárez-Enríquez, *Justicia Olvidada: La Impunidad de las Violaciones a Derechos Humanos cometidas por Soldados en México* (Washington Office on Latin America, November 2017), https://www.wola.org/es/analisis/informe-de-

wola-justicia-olvidada-la-impunidad-de-las-violaciones-derechos-humanos-cometidas-por-soldados-en-mexico/.

26. Human Rights Council, *Report of the Special Rapporteur on Torture and other Cruel, Inhuman or Degrading Treatment or Punishment, Juan E. Méndez. Addendum. Mission to Mexico* (December 29, 2014), U.N.Doc. A/HRC/28/68/Add.3 par. 76. The national and even the international press covered the rapporteur's concluding observations, including *The Guardian*'s article pointing out that '[a] scathing UN report has sharply rebuked Mexico for its widespread problem with torture … '. Jo Tuckman, 'UN: torture in Mexico occurs with "impunity" at hands of security forces', *The Guardian*, March 9, 2015, https://theguardian.com/world/2015/mar/09/mexico-torture-human-rights-violations-united-nations-report.
27. Inter-American Commission of Human Rights, Situation of Human Rights in Mexico (2015), OEA/Ser.L/V/II.Doc. 44/15. Carlos Fazio states that Mexico is going through a 'civilizatory crisis'. Carlos Fazio, *Estado de Emergencia. De la Guerra de Calderón a la Guerra de Peña Nieto* (Mexico City: Grijalbo, 2016).
28. Human Rights Council, *Report of the Special Rapporteur on Torture and other Cruel, Inhuman or Degrading Treatment or Punishment, Juan E. Méndez. Addendum. Mission to Mexico* (December 29, 2014), U.N.Doc. A/HRC/28/68/Add.3.
29. Human Rights Council, *Informe de seguimiento del Relator Especial sobre la tortura y otros tratos o penas crueles, inhumanos o degradantes – México* (February 17, 2017) U.N. Doc. A/HRC/34/54/Add.4, par. 104.
30. Committee against Torture, *Consideration of reports submitted by States parties under article 19 of the Convention*, México, U.N.Doc. A/48/44(Supp), par. 203.
31. Human Rights Council, *Report of the Special Rapporteur, Mr. Nigel S. Rodley, submitted pursuant to Commission on Human Rights resolution 1997/38. Addendum. Visit by the Special Rapporteur to Mexico* (January 14, 1998) U.N. Doc. E/CN.4/1998/38/Add.2, par. 7.
32. Centro de Derechos Humanos Miguel Agustín Pro Juárez, *Recomendaciones de Derechos Humanos al Estado Mexicano 2000–2010* (Mexico City: Centro de Derechos Humanos Miguel Agustín Pro Juárez, 2011), http://centroprodh.org.mx/index.php?option=com_docman&Itemid=28&lang=es&limitstart=25.
33. Committee against Torture, *Report of Mexico Produced by the Committee Under Article 20 of the Convention and Reply from the Government of Mexico* (May 27, 2003), U.N.Doc. CAT/C/75, par. 218.
34. Human Rights Council, *Report of the Special Rapporteur, Mr. Nigel S. Rodley, Submitted Pursuant to Commission on Human Rights Resolution 1997/38. Addendum. Visit by the Special Rapporteur to Mexico* (January 14, 1998) U.N. Doc. E/CN.4/1998/38/Add.2, par. 24.
35. Inter-American Commission of Human Rights, Situation of Human Rights in Mexico (2015), OEA/Ser.L/V/II.Doc. 44/15, par. 212.
36. Ibid.
37. Created in the year 1990 by presidential decree as a decentralised body of the Secretary of Government and transformed in 1992 into an autonomous constitutional body through a constitutional reform. National Human Rights Commission, 'Antecedentes', http://www.cndh.org.mx/Antecedentes (accessed October 29, 2018).
38. Some of them have to do with the obstacles mentioned by the Special Rapporteur on Torture in 2014, that is, unreported cases or cases classified as cruel, inhumane or degrading treatment ('ill-treatment' or CIDT). Another reason is competence: according to article 3 of the Commission's Law, it 'will have competence throughout the national territory, to hear complaints related to alleged human rights violations when these are imputed to federal authorities and public servants, with the exception of those belonging to the Federal Judicial Branch'. National Human Rights Commission Act (México) 1992, http://www.cndh.org.mx/sites/all/doc/normatividad/Ley_CNDH.pdf.
39. Mónica Beltrán Gaos, 'La protección descentralizada de los derechos humanos en México y en España', in *Derecho Constitucional. Memoria del Congreso Internacional de Culturas y Sistemas Jurídicos Comparados*, coord. Miguel Carbonell (Mexico City: UNAM, 2004), 147. The National Commission's Law established the latter's obligation to continue to receive

complaints involving local agents while human rights commissions were created by local legislatures. *See* National Human Rights Commission Act.

40. Beltrán, 'La protección descentralizada'; Pedrazzini, 'La represión del Estado', 18–19.
41. Pedrazzini, 'La represión del Estado', 18–19.
42. Ibid. The same author documented 1015 cases of 'aggression-injury', without specifying more information.
43. Comisión Mexicana de Defensa y Promoción de los Derechos Humanos, *Human Rights Violations in the Contexto f the War on Drugs* (Mexico City: Comisión Mexicana de Defensa y Promoción de los Derechos Humanos, 2015), http://www.cmdpdh.org/publicaciones-pdf/cmdpdh-violaciones-graves-a-ddhh-en-la-guerra-contra-las-drogas-en-mexico.pdf; Centro de Derechos Humanos Miguel Agustín Pro Juárez, Transición Traicionada. Los Derechos Humanos durante el Sexenio 2006–2012 (Mexico City: Centro de Derechos Humanos Miguel Agustín Pro Juárez, 2013); Human Rights Watch, *Neither Rights Nor Security*; ACAT-France, *Au nom de la 'guerre contre le crime'.* See also: Laura Carlsen, 'Mexico's False Dilemma: Human Rights or Security', *Northwestern Journal of International Human Rights* 10, no. 3 (2012); Instituto Belisario Domínguez Senado de la República, *Temas estratégicos 39. Seguridad Interior: Elementos para el Debate* (January 2017), http://www.bibliodigitalibd.senado.gob.mx/bitstream/handle/123456789/3344/Reporte39_SeguridadInterior_DistDigital.pdf?sequence=1&isAllowed=y.
44. Amnesty International, *México. Tortura e Impunidad: Reacciones del gobierno* (November 1991) AMR 41/17/91/s; Iván E. Saldaña 'Tortura no es una 'práctica generalizada' en México: SRE', *Excélsior*, March 9, 2015, https://www.excelsior.com.mx/nacional/2015/03/09/1012424; Rodrigo Aguilera, 'Mexico's Human Rights Challenge', *Huffington Post*, April 23, 2015, https://huffingtonpost.com/rodrigo-aguilera/mexicos-human-rights-chal_b_7131250.html; Unspecified autor, 'Relator de la ONU, irresponsable por dichos sobre tortura en México: SRE', *Expansión*, March 12, 2015, https://expansion.mx/nacional/2015/03/28/relator-de-la-onu-irresponsable-por-dichos-sobre-tortura-en-mexico-sre; Alejandro Pacheco, 'Pese a descalificaciones, relator contra la tortura de la ONU considera dar seguimiento a recomendaciones', *SDP Noticias,* April 1, 2015, https://sdpnoticias.com/nacional/2015/04/01/pese-a-descalificaciones-relator-contra-la-tortura-de-la-onu-considera-dar-seguimiento-a-recomendaciones.
45. Armando Meneses, 'Prohibición de la Tortura', in *Derechos Humanos en la Constitución: Comentarios de Jurisprudencia Constitucional e Interamericana*, Eduardo Ferrer MacGregor Poisot, José Luis Caballero Ochoa and Christian Steiner (México: SCJN, UNAM, Konrad Adenauer Stiftung, 2013).
46. Centro de Derechos Humanos Miguel Agustín Pro Juárez, *La Magnitud de la Crisis de Derechos Humanos en México*, 36; Naomi Larsson, 'Mexican government accused of torture and disabled care home', *The Guardian*, March 9, 2017, https://www.theguardian.com/global-development-professionals-network/2017/mar/09/ending-abuse-institutions-charity-case-mexican-government.
47. Amnesty International Mexico: Torture and Impunity, 7.
48. Ibid., 22.
49. Human Rights Council, *Report of the Special Rapporteur, Mr. Nigel S. Rodley, Submitted Pursuant to Commission on Human Rights Resolution 1997/38. Addendum. Visit by the Special Rapporteur to Mexico* (January 14, 1998) U.N. Doc. E/CN.4/1998/38/Add.2, par. 8.
50. CAT 2003, par. 137.
51. Human Rights Council, *Report of the Special Rapporteur on Torture and other Cruel, Inhuman or degrading treatment or punishment, Juan E. Méndez. Addendum. Mission to Mexico* (December 29, 2014), U.N.Doc. A/HRC/28/68/Add.3 par. 25.
52. Among said authorities are the federal Office of Prevention and Social Readaption and its state equivalent offices. National Human Rights Commission, *Annual Reports*, http://www.cndh.org.mx/Informes_Anuales_Actividades. Torture and maltreatment are also present in the context of the criminal enforcement system in Mexico, however it is many times invisible for several reasons, including the use of improper language meaning that maltreatment or

even torture by overcrowding is commonly referred to simply as 'prison overcrowding'. Miguel Sarre, email message to author, October 5, 2018.

53. National Human Rights Commission, *Annual Reports.*
54. In 1997 Amnesty International stated that '[c]onfessions continue to be considered the "queen of evidence" (la reina de las pruebas) in judicial proceedings'. Amnesty International, *Mexico. Amnesty International's Concerns regarding Torture and Ill-Treatment in Mexico* (April 1997) AMR 41/17/97, https://www.amnesty.org/download/Documents/160000/amr410171997en.pdf. Reports by national and international experts show the recurrence of this practice even nowadays. Centro de Derechos Humanos Miguel Agustín Pro Juárez, *La Magnitud de la Crisis de Derechos Humanos en México*, 55. Claudia Paz y Paz, 'Recomendaciones para mejorar el sistema de investigación criminal mexicano a la luz del caso Ayotzinapa', *Aportes DPLF*, 21, January 2017.
55. Committee against Torture, *Consideration of reports submitted by States parties under article 19 of the Convention*, México, U.N.Doc. A/48/44(Supp), par. 203.
56. Ibid.
57. Committee against Torture, *Report of Mexico Produced by the Committee under Article 20 of the Convention and Reply from the Government of Mexico* (May 27, 2003), U.N.Doc. CAT/C/75, par. 218.
58. Committee against Torture, *Concluding Observations on the Combined Fifth and Sixth Periodic Reports of Mexico as Adopted by the Committee at its Forty-ninth Session* (October 29–November 23, 2012), U.N.Doc. CAT/C/MEX/Q/5- 6, par. 10.
59. Human Rights Council, *Report of the Special Rapporteur on Torture and other Cruel, Inhuman or Degrading Treatment or Punishment, Juan E. Méndez. Addendum. Mission to Mexico* (December 29, 2014), U.N.Doc. A/HRC/28/68/Add.3, pars. 24–26.
60. Centro de Derechos Humanos Miguel Agustín Pro Juárez, *La Magnitud de la Crisis de Derechos Humanos en México*, 36.
61. Abel Miranda Ayala, 'Sin sustento científico la "Verdad Histórica"', *El Sur de Acapulco*, Septiembre 4, 2018, https://www.elsoldeacapulco.com.mx/local/estado/sin-sustento-cientifico-la-verdad-historica-1968569.html; Ariadna García, 'Tortura evidencia desaseo en caso Ayotzinapa: Vidulfo Rosales', *El Universal*, May 9, 2017, http://www.eluniversal.com.mx/articulo/nacion/sociedad/2017/05/9/tortura-evidencia-desaseo-en-caso-ayotzinapa-vidulfo-rosales; Redacción AN, 'Responde Centro Prodh a Peña: reprobada, la investigación de PGR sobre Ayotzinapa; faltan 'pruebas científicas irrebatibles', *Aristegui Noticias*, August 29, 2018, https://aristeguinoticias.com/2908/mexico/responde-centro-prodh-a-pena-reprobada-la-investigacion-de-pgr-sobre-ayotzinapa-faltan-pruebas-cientificas-irrebatibles/.
62. Claudia Paz y Paz, 'Recomendaciones para mejorar el sistema de investigación criminal mexicano a la luz del caso Ayotzinapa', *Aportes DPLF*, January 21, 2017; Alejandro Valencia Villa et al., *Informe Ayotzinapa II. Avances y Nuevas Conclusiones sobre la Investigación, Búsqueda y Atención a las Víctimas* (México City: Interdisciplinary Group of Independent Experts, 2016); Amnesty International, *Mexico. Amnesty International's Concerns regarding Torture and Ill-Treatment in Mexico* (April 1997) AMR 41/17/97, https://www.amnesty.org/download/Documents/160000/amr410171997en.pdf.
63. Human Rights Council, *Report of the Special Rapporteur on Torture and other Cruel, Inhuman or Degrading Treatment or Punishment, Juan E. Méndez. Addendum. Mission to Mexico* (December 29, 2014), U.N.Doc. A/HRC/28/68/Add.3, pars. 24–26.
64. Claudia Paz y Paz, 'Recomendaciones para mejorar el sistema de investigación criminal mexicano a la luz del caso Ayotzinapa', 6.
65. Stephanie E. Brewer, 'Hacia un proceso penal constitucional: Elementos para entender y aplicar la presunción de inocencia en México', *Revista del Instituto de la Judicatura Federal* 36 (2014), 145–147; 'DECLARACIONES DEL REO. INMEDIATEZ PROCESAL', Thesis IX.1o.6 P [TA], Nineth Period, T.C.C. [Collegiate Circuit Court], S.J.F. y su Gaceta [Weekly Federal Court Report], IV, July 1996, 385; 'PRINCIPIO DE INMEDIATEZ PROCESAL, INTERPRETACIÓN DEL. DIVERSAS DECLARACIONES DEL REO' [TA], Eighth

Period, T.C.C. [Collegiate Circuit Court], S.J.F. [Weekly Federal Court Report], VIII, August 1991, 206.

66. Brewer, 'Hacia un proceso penal constitucional', 145.
67. Ibid., 147.
68. 'CONFESIÓN, PLENO VALOR PROBATORIO DE LA', Thesis II.3o.J/20, Eighth Period, T.C.C. [Collegiate Circuit Court], S.J.F. y su Gaceta [Weekly Federal Court Report] 56, August 1992, 47; 'CONFESIÓN, SU VALOR PROBATORIO (LEGISLACIÓN PENAL FEDERAL)', Thesis VI.1o.J/100, Eighth Period, T.C.C. [Collegiate Circuit Court], Apéndice [Appendix] II, 1995, 295. The two court thesis cited here were upheld by the courts since 1989 and 1988, respectively.
69. 'PRUEBA CONFESIONAL, VALOR DE LA' [TA], Fifth Period, Third Chamber of the National Supreme Court of Justice, S.F.J. [Weekly Federal Court Report] CXXXI, Registry no. 338869, 1957, 133.
70. Judicial file Varios 912/2010, Ninth Period, Full Chamber of the National Supreme Court of Justice, S.J.F. y su Gaceta [Weekly Federal Court Report] Book I, October 2011, Volume 1, 313.
71. 'INMEDIATEZ PROCESAL. PRINCIPIOS QUE CONDICIONAN SU APLICACIÓN CUANDO EL INCULPADO SE RETRACTA DE UNA CONFESIÓN MINISTERIAL ALEGANDO QUE ÉSTA FUE OBTENIDA MEDIANTE ACTOS DE TORTURA', Thesis 1a. LVI/2017 (10ª.), Tenth Period, First Chamber of the National Supreme Court of Justice, S.J.F. [Weekly Federal Court Report] Book 42, May 2017, Volume I, 467.
72. Alejandro Valencia Villa et al., *Informe Ayotzinapa II,* 406.
73. Argentine Forensic Anthropology Team, Executive Summary [results on the study carried out at the garbage dump in Cocula, where federal authorities claimed that the bodies of the 43 disappeared students were burned] 2016, 18; Lizzie Wade, 'Were the bodies of the 43 missing students burned at a dumpsite?' *Science,* March 10, 2016, http://www.sciencemag.org/news/2016/03/were-bodies-43-missing-students-burned-dumpsite.
74. Kirk Semple, 'Missing Mexican Students Suffered a Night of "Terror", Investigators Say', *New York Times*, April 24, 2016, https://www.nytimes.com/2016/04/25/world/americas/missing-mexican-students-suffered-a-night-of-terror-investigators-say.html; Randal C. Archibold, '43 Missing Students, a Mass Grave and a Suspect: Mexico's Police', *New York Times*, October 6, 2014, https://www.nytimes.com/2014/10/07/world/americas/43-missing-students-a-mass-grave-and-a-suspect-mexicos-police-.html; ABC News, 'What we know about the 43 Missing Mexican Students', *ABC News*, October 24, 2014, https://abcnews.go.com/International/43-missing-mexican-students/story?id=26423875; Jo Tuckman, 'Mexico: Protests at Admission that 43 Missing Students Were Massacred', *The Guardian*, November 9, 2014, https://www.theguardian.com/world/2014/nov/09/mexico-demonstration-43-students-confirmed-massacred; Catherine E. Shoichet and Rafael Romo, 'Mexico's 43 Missing Students: Who are they?', *CNN*, November 14, 2014; No author specified, 'Missing Students Missing after Protest in Iguala', *BBC*, September 29, 2014, https://www.bbc.com/news/world-latin-america-29406630.
75. Alejandro Valencia Villa et al., *Informe Ayotzinapa II,* 582.
76. Tomuschat, 'Democracy and the Rule of Law', 474; Peerenboom, 'Human Rights and Rule of Law'.
77. Ibid., 475.
78. Ibid.
79. Peerenboom, 'Human Rights and Rule of Law', 20.
80. Evan Fox-Decent, 'Is the rule of law really indifferent to human rights?', *Law and Philosophy* 27 (2008): 534.
81. World Justice Project, 'Rule of Law Index 2017–2018', https://worldjusticeproject.org/sites/default/files/documents/WJP-ROLI-2018-June-Online-Edition_0.pdf.
82. Peerenbom, 'Human Rights and Rule of Law', 21. The author states that a free-market economy is one of the conditions, but one may question if the same would be true where there is a social democratic approach to the market place.

83. Report of the Secretary General, *The Rule of Law and Transitional Justice in Conflict and Post-conflict Societies* (August 23, 2004) U.N.Doc. S/2004/616, par. 6.
84. Arturo Ángel, 'En 2018 Jueces desechan el 80% de los casos que envía la PGR; seis veces más que al inicio del sexenio', *Animal Político,* September 5, 2018, https://www.animalpolitico.com/2018/09/jueces-casos-desechados-pgr-sexenio/.
85. Ibid.
86. An analysis regarding what has changed in judicial practice is out of the limits of this article, but possible explanations may be found in the 2011 constitutional reform, which may be finally permeating in the courts and operating as the mechanism that allows the 'translation' or application of international standards into national judicial practice. Centro de Derechos Humanos Miguel Agustín Pro Juárez, Instituto Mexicano de Derechos Humanos y Democracia y Programa de Derechos Humanos de la Universidad Iberoamericana Ciudad de México, *Del Papel a la Práctica: La Aplicación de las Reformas Constitucionales en el Sistema de Justicia 2011–2016* (Mexico City, 2017).
87. World Justice Project, 'Rule of Law Index 2017–2018', http://data.worldjusticeproject.org/.
88. Arturo Ángel, 'La cero efectividad de PGR de esclarecer homicidios: en 8 años obtuvo dos sentencias', *Animal Político*, August 16, 2018, https://www.animalpolitico.com/2018/08/la-cero-efectividad-de-pgr-para-esclarecer-homicidios-en-8-anos-obtuvo-dos-sentencias/.
89. Committee on Enforced Disappearances, *Concluding Observations on the Report submitted by Mexico Under Article 29, Paragraph 1, of the Convention* (March 5, 2015) U.N. Doc. CED/C/Mex/CO/1, par. 10.
90. Judgment 'Amparo en revisión 203/2017', 'First Collegiate Circuit Court of the 19th Circuit', June 4, 2018 par. 1096.
91. OHCHR, *Manual on the Effective Investigation and Documentation of Torture and Other Cruel, Inhuman or Degrading Treatment or Punishment ("Istanbul Protocol")* (2004) U.N. Doc. HR/P/PT/8/Rev.1.
92. Judgment 'Amparo en revisión 203/2017'.

Acknowledgments

I am very grateful with Professor Miguel Sarre for his valuable comments; Professor Francisco Calderón for his orientation when analyzing the data and Professor Irving Rosales for his general guidance and motivation. I also wish to thank Law student Ricardo Becerra, who assisted me on part of the research.

Disclosure statement

No potential conflict of interest was reported by the author.

ORCID

Denise González-Núñez http://orcid.org/0000-0002-1259-7946

EU membership conditionality in promoting acceptance of peremptory human rights norms: a case study in Albania considering public opinion

Ridvan Peshkopia, Drin Konjufca, Erblin Salihu and Jonida Lika

ABSTRACT

Since its inception, European Union membership conditionality has played a major role in bringing EU candidate countries from former communist Eastern Europe in line with international human rights norms. In spite of such progress, those societies harbour significant inconsistencies in both their perception of what constitutes human rights and the role public trust in domestic and international actors plays in those perceptions. By highlighting those inconsistencies and discussing their origins, this paper aims at filling an explanatory gap related to instances when we should expect that EU membership conditionality would serve as an agent of human rights *jus cogens*, and when it would fail to do so. By relying on a probability simple random sample of public opinion data that we collected in Albania in 2016, we test our propositions with the case of people's support for ethnic minority rights, homosexual rights, Syrian refugees seeking asylum in Albania, women's rights and the reinstatement of the death penalty.

Introduction

How effective are international actors in spreading certain human rights as *jus cogens* (also known as peremptory norms) in non-Western societies? As one of those actors focused on spreading human rights norms in its neighbourhood and across the globe, is the EU effective in conditioning membership with appropriation of the human rights *jus cogens*? Focused on their very nature, their definition and their source, the debate over the conceptualising of human rights norms as *jus cogens* or customary has overlooked people's perceptions of those norms.[1] People's perception of norm hierarchy is important because it impacts society's ability and capability to comply with emerging international human rights norms.[2] The lack of systematic empirical analysis concerning factors that impact people's acceptation of human rights as *jus cogens* prevents us from knowing the role of socioeconomic and socio-psychological factors arguably relevant in human rights socialisation. Moreover, the mass level of analysis and the individual as an analytic unit are often overlooked in favour of meso- and macro theories,[3] and sometimes even the domestic sociopolitical and cultural context is taken as unified and static. Whereas only recently do we have a list of peremptory human rights norms, local societies might still exhibit differences in what they embrace as human rights *jus cogens* and what they perceive to be simply public policies in service of a specific public purpose.

Trying to empirically bring the individual into the debate, we hope to contribute to a growing body of research that inquires into people's attitudes toward human rights. This becomes even more important since, recently embedded in natural law thinking, human rights as *jus cogens* seems disassociated from the project of international cooperation, and asserts rather the primacy of the individual.[4] Individuals and groups are supposed to be impacted by virtue of harm to peremptory norms and yet, only relatively recently are they emerging along sovereign states as parts of the international jurisprudence.[5] Individuals are regarded as 'the ultimate beneficiaries and in that sense as the holders of the relevant rights'.[6] Therefore, opening up international human rights jurisprudence to individuals and groups by introducing peremptory human rights norms begs the question of how individuals and groups perceive peremptory human rights norms as well as what mechanisms are at play to socialise societies with this emerging hierarchy of international norms.

We inquire into the EU's capability to convey human rights as *jus cogens* to EU membership aspiring countries. Focusing on Albania, we empirically inquire into the role of EU membership conditionality on institutionalising and integrating into society a set of human rights, namely support for women, ethnic minority, homosexual and refugee rights as well as attitudes toward the reinstatement of capital punishment. Analyzing historic facts, official documents, newspaper reports and public opinion data, we analyze the impact of EU membership conditionality on human rights policies and practices in Albania. We argue that, whereas EU membership conditionality might successfully impact institutionalisation of human rights, it might not always succeed in making societies adequately integrate those norms. On the view of the current authors EU membership conditionality is the most powerful tool at the European Union's disposal toward policy change in EU membership aspiring countries,[7] and the entire post-communist transformation considered as the complex process of the return to Europe. We argue that people's attitudes toward EU membership conditionality might also serve as a litmus test regarding which human rights stipulated by the EU through EU membership conditionality have been embraced by local publics, and which human rights people refuse to embrace. If our argument holds, we should see an association between people's view of EU membership conditionality as helping a country's democratisation and support for women, ethnic minority, homosexual and refugee rights – rights that have been listed as *jus cogens* and explicitly deployed through EU membership conditionality.[8] By the same token, we should not expect the same association between people's view of EU membership conditionality as helping a country's democratisation and their support for the death penalty, since people might not see the abolition of the death penalty as a human rights issue, albeit stipulated by the EU as a must for countries seeking to join the Union. Indeed, we find evidence that people positively associate their beliefs that EU membership conditions help democratisation with higher support for women, ethnic minority, homosexual and Syrian refugee protection. However, we find no evidence of any association between people's beliefs that EU membership conditions help democratisation and level of people's support for the reinstatement of the death penalty. Those findings indicate that people are receptive only to some of the EU-promoted human rights, but not necessarily to all of them. Those findings could be instructive about the power and limitations of EU membership conditionality as an agent of human rights as *jus cogens*.

Human rights as *jus cogens*

Peremptory norms (*jus cogens*), formulated in the Vienna Convention on the Law of Treaties, refer to 'compelling law', as the technical term given to those norms of general international law that are argued to be hierarchically superior.[9] The Vienna Convention defines the source of *jus cogens* or peremptory norms as the will of the international community on the ground that it is a non-derogable norm 'accepted and recognised by the international community of states as a whole'.[10] Judicial decisions and scholarly thinking are increasingly referring to the common interest of mankind to identify overarching concerns underpinning international public policies, but also to the international community as an authority of collective action.[11] Peremptory norms are emerging either as a new non-consensual source of legal obligation or as a consensual identification of certain norms in positive law of a higher hierarchic order than other norms.[12] In practice, peremptory norms assert themselves in two ways: first, they trump other norms of the international law, especially customary immunity; second, they are imposed on a persistent objector or in a national system which does not give supremacy to 'ordinary' international law.[13]

Therefore, peremptory norms are said to possess a universal character in that no state may derogate from them, even if peremptory norms conflict with customary norms, general principles of international law, and treaty provisions.[14] Human rights *jus cogens* had been largely developed by international legal scholarship even before its sanctioning by judicial decisions in the 1990s.[15] Perceptively, there is a tendency to elevate human rights in the *jus cogens* category.[16] Recent literature argues that there is an almost intrinsic relationship between peremptory norms and human rights, and that most of the case law in which the concept of *jus cogens* has been invoked is taken up with human rights.[17] The UN Charter, a source of supranational authority, assigns, on the view of some if not all states and as reflected in their practice, national sovereignty as the ultimate principle of international law, and assigns human rights a subordinate position in the overall scheme. Consequentially, in arguing for human rights as *jus cogens*, human rights-oriented scholars are drawing from natural law as an implicit source of higher authority.[18] Therefore, human rights do not derive from the will of states, but are inalienable or inherent.[19] Indeed, the most important challenge to even categorising human rights as *jus cogens* is state sovereignty, and the prevailing of the former over the latter would mean setting human rights as the ultimate international law principle.[20] Since there is currently no international court to administer international human rights law, jurisdictions of different international courts and tribunals extend over only specific aspects of world regions.[21] Most of those mechanisms depend on the willingness of states to abide by their authority, and human rights as *jus cogens* might represent a legal instrument to overcome state sovereignty as the fundamental principle of international law.[22]

Critics of the human rights as *jus cogens* point out that in spite of their acknowledged peremptory status, thus far no human rights instrument indisputably refers to peremptory norms,[23] and we lack a concise list of peremptory human rights norms.[24] In the words of its critics, *jus cogens* has had few practical uses, and its legal consequences seldom apply to any actual legal problem; most often, there is no objector to be bound against its will, no offending treaty provision to be voided; no exorbitant countermeasure to be condemned as a wrongful derogation, and no 'illegal situation' to be denied recognition.[25] Even authors sympathetic to the categorisation of human rights as *jus cogens* fail to find human rights as peremptory norms outside the EU Charter, clearly a customary law. Arguably, it is difficult to show, beyond any doubt and referencing international law authority, which human rights norms represent *jus cogens*.[26] In the cases when authors have pointed at some of those norms, they have failed to demonstrate their being exclusively peremptory norms, as they have been recognised as simultaneously being *jus cogens* norms, core and non-derogable rights, and as obligations *erga omnes* such as are equality and non-discrimination, the right to life, the right to be free from slavery, and the right to be free form torture, together with fundamental judicial protections necessary to ensure the enjoyment of other rights.[27]

EU membership conditionality as an agent of human rights as *jus cogens*

Human rights as a condition for EU membership appeared first with the 1992 Lisbon European Council, when the Commission asserted the importance of 'democratic status and respect of human rights as basic conditions for membership'. The former communist countries from Eastern Europe that have embarked on political and economic reforms to transform societies after over four decades of communism have to fulfil the so called 'Copenhagen criteria' in order to qualify for EU membership. That policy would prevent the EU from starting negotiations with a country if the latter has unsatisfactory records of complying with EU expectations on democratic conditions, the respect for human rights and minority protection. Human rights conditionality for accession are formally stipulated in two separate EU texts: the 'political criteria' established by the European Council in Copenhagen 1993, and Article 49 of the Treaty on European Union (TEU), another Amsterdam innovation. Thus, ironically, the very 1993 Copenhagen criteria that the EU deployed to membership aspiring countries from former communist Eastern Europe were drawn even before the EU had its own overarching human rights text.

The EU represents a case of shifting from one ignoring human rights to one being 'founded on [...] respect for human rights and fundamental freedoms'.[28] The difficulties of reaching an overarching consensus about the either universal or parochial nature of human rights has plagued the European Union for a long time.[29] Therefore, uncertainties about the scope of human rights in European law and practice has made the application of these principles problematic as they remain grounded within the EU legal order.[30] Indeed, the idea to draw up a Charter of Fundamental Rights first emerged at the 1999 Cologne European Council, but the Charter has overlapping rights with the European Convention and was promulgated on 7 December 2000 by the European Parliament, the Council of Human Rights Ministers and the European Commission. However, after the EU had finally created its own bill of rights, the latter was not compulsory.[31] The Charter was incorporated into the 1997 Amsterdam Treaty (TEU), with its Article 2 explicitly noting human rights as a founding principle, of the European Union.[32] Moreover, by virtue of Art. 6 (1) of TEU as amended by the Lisbon Treaty, the Charter became part of the primary law of the EU.[33] Article 6 (2) provides for the EU to accede to the European Convention on Human Rights; and the European Court of Justice (CJEU) is to have greater powers of judicial review in the field of police and judicial cooperation in criminal law, an area of obvious relevance to human rights.[34] Arguably, it is exactly the transformation of the Charter into a legally binding document with primary law status, and the extension of the Court's jurisdiction in areas such as asylum, immigration and criminal matters, which in particular have increased the Court's profile in the fundamental rights field, and resulted in elevating human rights as *just cogens*.[35]

The case of the EU is interesting to analyze because, within the Copenhagen criteria, implicitly the EU introduced human rights as a criteria of a higher order, although the rights were not codified as customary law by the EU itself. Even before human rights could become part of the EU customary laws, they appeared as higher ranking norms in the EU relations with former communist countries from Eastern Europe aspiring EU membership. And since *jus cogens* norms give human rights legal universality necessary for their implementation,[36] one can argue that siding with the universality of human rights norms offers the EU more leverage to apply it as a condition in its eastward enlargement.

EU membership conditionality as a tool to enforce human rights

EU membership conditionality can be defined as the set of conditions stipulated by the EU for EU membership aspiring countries for implementing reforms and pursuing policies in the direction prescribed by the Union.[37] The latter articulates the set of conditions imposed by the EU on membership aspiring countries in order for them to meet the EU membership criteria, known as *acquis communitaire*. Such conditions require the applicants to build a functioning market economy; ensure the stability of institutions established to guarantee democracy, the rule of law, human rights, and respect for and protection of minorities; and bolster capacity to take on obligations of EU membership in regards to economic and political solutions. Applied in the Balkans, EU membership conditionality serves as a multidimensional and multi-purpose instrument geared toward reconciliation, reconstruction and reform; it is regional, sub-regional, bilateral and project-specific and relates to economic, political, social and security-related criteria.[38] There is a joint sense among the EU and former communist countries from Southeastern Europe that EU accession and transition to democracy and a market-oriented economy are part of the same process, and preparation to join the EU is conterminous with overall development goals.[39] From the demand-side viewpoint, conditionality could minimise the risk of new entrants becoming politically unstable and economically burdensome to the existing EU members.[40] From the supply-side approach, EU conditions and the programmes attached to them provide material support for implementing reforms; shield moderate politics from populism and nationalism; strengthen democratic forces in the face of authoritarian downturns; and serve as instrumental justification for domestic policies that Eastern European leaders need to implement to attain their own rational, power-driven goals.[41] EU membership conditions provide EU membership aspiring countries with political and economic objectives as well as guidelines for achieving these objectives. The perspective of membership in the EU has created powerful incentives as transition states shape their reforms.[42]

EU membership conditionality's success rests on an obvious asymmetry of interdependence in EU conditionality.[43] This asymmetry reflects both the high priority that EU membership represents to EU membership aspiring countries from former communist Eastern Europe and low public support for enlargement in current EU members countries.[44] The economic and political benefits expected with EU membership, the lack of equivalent alternatives for post-communist EECs (Eastern European Countries), and the weak interest of the EU in eastward political enlargement make EU membership conditionality a particularly powerful tool in the hands of the EU during its negotiations for eastward expansion.[45] Whereas EU member states and EECs will both benefit from EU enlargement, new members are expected to benefit more, thus putting the latter at a disadvantage in bargaining.[46]

Whereas extant research shows that EU membership conditionality could effectively affect policy change in certain reforms, its results might not be so bold in other reforms.[47] Lack of tangible short-term benefits as well as incentives sufficient for reforms, and even a lack of EU interest to bring about such domestic social change might negatively affect reform progress.[48] EU engagement to impact domestic social change becomes even more important when social change would mean changing social behaviour not only of elites, but also of society at large. Arguably, legislating and implementing human rights reforms or other institutional reforms that impact a country's human rights culture potentially could lead to human rights norm institutionalisation. However, norm socialisation does not happen unless the most important societal actors, including the public at large appropriate that norm.[49] Deploying EU membership conditionality to acquire the acquiescence of the elites is always easier than engaging in meaningful campaigns to socialise masses with EU advocated human rights norms, and usually the EU does not undertake such an exercise.[50] Instead, the EU defers such a task to domestic elites, and holds them accountable for EU-imposed human rights socialisation.[51]

Therefore, we still don't know to what a degree people in the receiving countries are responsive to EU membership conditionality as an agent of human rights proliferation. Previous research has shown that citizens of Balkan countries aspiring to join the EU are resisting the abolition of the death penalty, and much evidence shows that women's and homosexuals' rights violations are widespread. We argue that, whereas people associate women, ethnic minority, homosexual and refugee rights with the EU and EU membership, they might not make a direct link between the death penalty and the right for life with EU membership conditionality as an agent of such a norm. Next follows an empirical case study of that question conducted in Albania.

Study case and hypotheses

We build and test a number of hypotheses with the case of Albanians' attitudes toward women, ethnic minority, homosexual and refugee rights as well as their attitudes toward death penalty restoration. The case is instructive in several aspects. First, after almost half a century of communist self-isolation, Albania is trying to catch up with the rest of the world, but Albania and Albanians continue to remain understudied cases. Albania's overture toward the rest of the world presents the country with both opportunities and challenges in grappling with new ideas and norms. Second, in spite of its maverick brand of communism, during the Cold War the country shared similarities with other communist countries that stemmed from their ideological affiliation with the Soviet Bloc and a Soviet-style society, which would help generalisation of our findings over smaller maverick systems still existing in the former Soviet geopolitical space.[52] Third, with the collapse of communism in late 1990, Albania began its path to democratisation, economic liberalisation and EU membership. The journey turned out to be much harder than anticipated: the EU finally agreed to open negotiations for the Stabilization and Association Agreement with Albania in January 2006, and the visa liberalisation agreement with the Schengen area countries was reached in the fall of 2010. However, from 2010, when Albania first applied for EU membership, until 2012, when it acquired its EU candidate country status, the EU has rejected Albania's requests not once but thrice, making its applications the first one to have been formally rejected by the EU thus far, based mainly on the lack of progress in institutional reforms and a notorious lack of willingness of opposing parties to cooperate on those reforms. During this period, domestic and foreign observers alike have observed the strong support among the Albanians for their country's EU membership. However, the country continues to score a modest record in international human rights ranking, in spite of having signed and ratified almost every major international convention related to human rights.[53] An inquiry into the EU-Albania dynamics over human rights would elucidate advantages and limitations of EU membership conditionality in enforcing human rights as *jus cogens* in EU membership aspiring countries from Southeast Europe.

Women rights

Due to striking similarities, often women rights in the Balkans countries aspiring to EU membership are discussed as a common issue. The EU membership objective has had a positive impact as the Balkans have aligned relevant legislation with the highest EU and international standards.[54] The problem remains with practical implementations; in practical terms countries tend to overlook gender equality in order to pay attention to economic and political issues. Low levels of implementation of existing laws has prevented social change in favour of a growing role of women in their societies. For some authors, the biggest challenge for improving gender equality is changing the mentality of both women and men towards traditional gender roles.[55] The European Commission's Albania 2018 Report points out that a number of laws still contain gender-discriminatory provisions and encourages Albanian authorities to undertake further efforts to ensure that all strategies and policies are gender mainstreamed.[56] However, on a positive note, the 2017 World Economic Forum Gender Gap Index report showed that Albania improved compared to 2016 (rising from a ranking of 62–38 of 144 countries). Commenting on its own Albania 2018 Report, the European Commission's noted that its critique toward women rights in Albania is limited to the poor state of institutional mechanisms to protect the rights of the child and to tackle gender-based violence which remain poor.[57] Therefore, Albania society's efforts to improve women rights in the country align with the EU's concerns toward fulfilling such a condition, and *we should expect that people's support for women rights will statistically associate with their perception of EU membership conditionality being helpful to democratization of Albania.*

Ethnic minority rights

In June 2014, Albania acquired the EU candidate status. In its October 2014 Progress Report, the EU Commission considered the European Council's decision to grant Albania candidate status as 'recognition for the reform steps undertaken', and 'an encouragement to step up the pace of reforms'.[58] The only sentence addressing further efforts that the country needed to put in order to further progress toward full EU membership was: 'Albania will need to focus on implementing measures to enhance Roma inclusion and protect vulnerable groups'. By the same token, a European Commissions press release recognises that '[i]mportant steps were made to improve the legal framework for the respect for and protection of minorities but relevant secondary legislation needs to be developed'.[59] Compared to other problematic issues, such a narrow focus shows that the EU seems reasonably satisfied with Albania's progress in respecting ethnic minorities. That progress has been facilitated also by the fact that Albania is largely an ethnically homogenous society, with censuses persistently showing those who claim to belong to any other ethnicity than Albanian range between 1.58% and 2.5% of the population.[60]

Even during communism, Albania did show some formal recognition of ethnic minorities with non-discrimination clauses in the Albanian communist constitutional provisions of 1950.[61] That lip service to minority rights notwithstanding, from 1944 until the fall of communism in the late 1990, the Greek minority suffered human rights violations, as did virtually the entire Albanian population.[62] With the collapse of communism, Albania has undertaken a number of commitments to align its minority rights protection with the international law. Since 1991, Albania is a member of the International Covenant on Civil and Political Rights, wherein Article 27 sanctions for ethnic minority group rights. Since 2000, Albania has been implementing the Council of Europe's Framework Convention for the Protection of National Minorities, which subjects the country to progress monitoring. The latter highlight special measures for minority cultures, but not all of those measures concern discrimination.[63] Albania has yet to sign and ratify the European Charter for Regional or Minority Languages, the ratification of which is mandatory in the frame of EU accession, as well as sign and ratify UN's OHCHR Declaration of the Rights of Persons Belonging to National or Ethnic, Religious and Linguistic Minorities. Most importantly, Albania's Stabilizations and Association Agreement with the EU also provides for the protection of the rights of persons belonging to minorities.

Although the official number of national minorities in Albania is nine, the ethnic Greek minority are the only minority in Albania large enough to have political, economic and social significance. The fate of that minority has impacted much of the Albanian-Greek relations during the last 100 years. Greece has not shied away from its veto power in the EU to impact policy change in the country, especially during the 1990s.[64] However, both countries have grown increasingly pragmatic in their bilateral relations, as both understand their vital need for thriving economic relations as well as peace and stability. Therefore, in spite of brief periods of crisis flaring up here and there, mainstream politics in both countries have succeeded in marginalising nationalist and opportunistic politicians in favour of a working relationship between both countries.[65] As a result, now issues with ethnic minority rights in Albania seem more related to the preservation of their cultural heritage rather than a more fulsome effort to protect a range of human rights, although insufficient efforts to preserve ethnic minorities' cultural heritage also seems to plague the entire Southeast Europe.[66] According to an argument, especially in protecting ethnic minorities' cultural heritage, the problem rests mainly with Albanian authorities' hands-off approach, and that Albania's integrationist/assimilationist policy of non-discrimination (neither positive nor negative) towards ethnic and cultural minorities has led to the gradual fading out of minority cultural heritage and identity, and efforts of foreign actors to step in to fill the void.[67] Based on this review, we can conclude that Albania's steady efforts to align its protection of ethnic minority rights with EU best practices shows a social coalescence fulfilling this specific EU condition, and *we should expect people's support for ethnic minority rights to statistically associate with their perception of EU membership conditionality as being helpful to democratization of Albania.*

Homosexual rights

The communist legislation related to homosexuality reflected the Bolshevik conservative tradition on the issue, which considered homosexuals an alien part of society in the best case, and criminals in the worst case. During its 46 years of existence, the Albanian communist regime and the entire Albanian society took extremely aggressive positions against homosexuality, including long prison terms, systemic bullying, ostracising and isolation. Indeed, oppressing and suppressing homosexuals was one of the very few issues where the regime and the Albanian society largely synced.[68] Post-socialist Albania carried that tradition, and homosexuality as a crime continued to appear in the Penal Code even after its amendments in 1994, albeit with prison time reduced from ten years to just three. In January 1995, as Albania was preparing for the Council of Europe membership, the *Kuvend* adopted the new Penal Code, decriminalising homosexuality, promulgating sexual freedom, and introducing sexual crimes with Section VI, under Chapter II, Criminal Acts against the Individual and Crimes against Life. In 2006, the Albanian Human Rights Group began to draw up the Antidiscrimination Law, aiming to protect marginalised individuals and persons belonging to minority groups. The law, which intended to help fulfil the EU acquis was adopted by the *Kuvend* (the Albanian parliament) in February 2007 as Law 10221 on the Protection against Discrimination. The Law provided for the establishment of the Office of the Commissioner for Protection from Discrimination. Among others, the Antidiscrimination Law provides for the protection of the LGBT community in several socioeconomic aspects, including employment and education in the public and private sector.[69]

The fact that the post-socialist Albania carried homosexuality as a crime until half a decade after the communist collapse in 1990 reflects the traditionally hostile approach of Albanian political elites and the public at large toward homosexuality.[70] Even after the decriminalisation of homosexuality in 1995, widespread hostility against homosexuals had created a suppressive social condition which prevented the emergence of gay identity as a distinct social identity. However, by the second half of the 1990s, the Society Gay Albania (SGA), secretly created in 1993, began to come out, albeit by concealing its members' identities. Testimonies of Albanian homosexuals attempted to bring attention to the difficulties of gay life in Albania. Shadowed interviews with gay activists showed that, legal changes notwithstanding, homosexuals in Albania continued to suffer exclusion from state institutions as well as marginalisation, harassment and violence at the hands of police and by the public at large. Besides being ostracised form society, Albanian homosexuals often feel marginalised by their own families as the Albania social culture considers homosexuality to be shameful. For many years, most human rights nongovernment organisations (NGOs) focusing on human rights, mostly avoided the issue. However, two new LGBT associations created after 1996 helped growing awareness of the plight of the gay community in Albania. Meanwhile, the Albanian media has taken a primarily sensational approach to homosexual rights, publishing stories that would increase ratings and circulation, but doing little to promote social change in the area of gay rights protection.[71]

In June 2009, then Premier Sali Berisha shocked the Albanian society when he declared that his government would submit a bill providing for same sex marriage. Although that promise never materialised, the opening of the debate encouraged gay rights advocacy, and three more gay associations were created. Berisha iterated his support for gay rights in a speech in *Kuvend*, and also rebuked some government junior partners for their extreme positions against the gay community. Berisha repeated his support for gay rights in a meeting with representatives of the gay community in April 2013.[72] Moreover, the new government majority stemming from the 2013 parliamentary elections seemed friendlier toward the gay community. However, the short romance between Prime Minister Edi Rama and gay rights advocates suffered in summer 2016 when the government sponsored bill, part of a package of constitutional reform, dropped the same sex marriage clause, after meeting fierce resistance from a group of parliamentarians, key to achieving the 3/5 majority to instigate constitutional amendments.[73]

Support by two latest Premiers notwithstanding, Albanians' attitudes toward gay rights seem to change painfully slowly. The situation has improved somehow lately as in 2017 the Albanian LGBT community managed to peacefully have their parade in Tirana, a far cry from the protests that attempts to gay parade experienced in 2012.[74] This brief report shows that, in spite of initial dilemmas and unsteady efforts, finally Albanian society is working toward aligning its protection of homosexual rights with EU best practices, and *we should expect that people's support for homosexual rights will statistically associate with their perception of EU membership conditionality being helpful to democratization of Albania.*

Refugee rights

Legal and institutional capacities of refugee protection in EU membership aspiring countries from former communist Eastern Europe have been built and developed under pressure from EU conditionality.[75] Until the 2005 Hague Programme Action Plan and the 2007 Green Paper on the Future of the European Asylum System, EU membership conditionality was aimed at assisting former communist countries from Eastern Europe to set asylum systems compatible with the 1951 Geneva Convention on the Refugee Status. However, with the 2007 Green Paper, it became clearer that the EU expects from its aspirants the establishment of asylum systems that would contribute to solidarity and burden sharing. In order to be able to carry out such a task, EU membership aspiring countries must establish refugee rights consistent with the common European asylum policy. However, in some of the EU membership aspiring countries, Albania included, these institutions continue not to serve any domestic need, as the country does not experience significant numbers of refugees seeking protection.[76]

For the postsocialist Balkans countries, developing asylum systems became part of the Stabilization and Association Agreements (SAA) from the launch of the Stabilization and Association Programme (SAP), May 1999, and rests in the chapter on justice and home affairs. The Treaty of Amsterdam, 1997, envisions the EU as an area of freedom and security. As such, the EU views its enlargement as expanding this area, and requires the EU membership aspiring countries to develop laws, institutions, and rules compatible with those that underpin and promote EU freedom and security. The Balkans are located on the Balkan Route, the transit route of illegal immigrants from the Middle East and Central and Eastern Asia to the EU territory.[77] Countless illegal economic migrants, mainly from Eastern Turkey, Iraq, Iran, Pakistan and China, have transited the Balkans toward EU countries during the last three decades.[78] Since few of the illegal migrants and refugees are interested in staying in the Balkans, but simply transit through its countries toward the EU, the governments in the region did not make a serious effort to thwart this influx. Arguably, for the newly emerging democracies in Eastern Europe, institutional reforms in the area of asylum add strain in their already weak economies and social welfare systems.[79]

During the last three decades, Albania has experienced a 'migration explosion', with hundreds of thousands of Albanians leaving the country for a better life in neighbouring countries or elsewhere in the West.[80] That outward move has impacted the Albanian population in such a dramatic way that, once the fastest growing population in Europe is now in almost two-decades of decline.[81] With the exception of a brief period in spring 1999, when Albania hosted almost half a million Kosovo Albanian refugees,[82] refugees from the Middle and Far East on their way to Western Europe have tried to bypass Albania thus far.[83] Ever since it signed the 1951 Geneva Convention, Albania has fulfilled all its obligations toward building a refugee protection system, but over time Albania's asylum system has shown that it is good only in paper, and that it has not offered any significant contribution to the European common asylum policy.[84]

The refugee crisis tends to provoke negative reactions associated with fears of terrorism and national identity erosion.[85] By having greater access to the mass media, politicians play a significant role in shaping the public discourse related to immigration and refugees, thus directly impacting public opinion on this issue.[86] Such capability to cue the general public would mean that politicians transfer to the masses their growing anti-immigrant sentiments, causing higher levels of nationalism among the public.[87] However, combining elite compliance with EU demands with low numbers of refugees seeking protection in Albania, *we should expect that people's support for refugee rights (in the form of support for Syrian refugees to settle in Albania) will statistically associate with their perception of EU membership conditionality being helpful to democratization of Albania.*

The abolition of the death penalty

The Penal Code of the People's Socialist Republic of Albania promulgated the death penalty for a series of crimes, including crimes against the state. With the demise of the communist regime during 1990–1991, Albania dropped capital punishment for political crimes, but the death penalty still featured in seven articles of the new penal code introduced in 1995. The same year Albania's permanent membership in the Council of Europe (CoE) was conditional on the abolition of the death penalty, a step that the country was unprepared to undertake. However, the country acceded to the CoE and committed itself to sign, ratify and apply Protocol No. 6 within three years of accession and to immediately place a moratorium on executions until the total abolition of capital punishment. However, in 1996–1997 the country underwent social unrest, as hundreds of thousands of guns and other weapons were looted from military depots, and chaos spread around the country.[88]

As Albania began to restore order, the issue of the death penalty was reopened along with the process to draft a new constitution. The public at large and several prominent politicians were firmly in support of the death penalty. CoE and EU pressure grew as the country was approaching the end of the execution moratorium, and the draft of the first post-Communist constitution did not abolish outright the death penalty. With a popular majority in favour of the death penalty, there was always the risk of a referendum rejection of the bill without the death penalty.[89] Therefore, the drafting Commission adopted a neutral approach by proposing a constitutional article that asserted: 'The life of the person is protected by law'. Such an ambiguous text became a point of legal and political contention as Arben Imami, then Minister for Legislative Reform and Co-Chair of the Commission for Drafting the Project-Constitution, and Thimio Kondi, then Minister of Justice, argued that 'the Constitution does neither allow nor avoid the death penalty'. On the other side, representatives of the political opposition Spartak Ngjela, but also the government nominated Prosecutor General Albert Rakipi stated that the Constitution prohibits the death penalty.[90]

The new constitution passed in a referendum in November 1998, leaving open the issue on whether or not it allowed for the death penalty. The President was constrained to order the executions, whereas there were no tangible possibilities that Albanian legislative, *Kuvend*, would amend the Penal Code by removing the death penalty. In such a situation, the CoE expanded its role by consulting the Venice Commission on the compatibility of the death penalty with the Constitution of Albania. At its 38th plenary meeting on 22–23 March, the Venice Commission adopted an Opinion in which it found that 'the death penalty was incompatible with the new Albanian Constitution'.[91] By the end of 1999, the Constitutional Court opened the case on the interpretation of Article 21 of the Constitution, following a request by country's Supreme Court. In its Decision No. 65, 10 December 1999, the Constitutional Court judged unanimously the retention of the death penalty in peace time as incompatible with the Constitution of the Republic of Albania.[92] In May 2003, Albania signed the Protocol No. 13 to the Convention for the Protection of Human Rights and Fundamental Freedoms, concerning the abolition of death penalty in all circumstances, but it took almost four years for the *Kuvend* to ratify it in 2007.

The abolition of the death penalty in the former communist Eastern Europe happened either by parliamentary decision or by court decisions – in both cases, by active efforts to keep the public as far as possible from the debate.[93] However, even almost two decades after the abolition of the death penalty, the issue has not disappeared from public attention.[94] The Albanian media zealously reflects the rage of people affected by crime, thus, implicitly, being a persistent supporter of the death penalty restoration.[95] Some of the parliamentary political parties still retain the death penalty in their manifestos, and public opinion seems restless in its demands to restore the death penalty. Recently even the chief of the opposition has promised to hold a referendum over the death penalty reinstatement should his coalition win the next parliamentary elections.[96] Such a major discrepancy among various political and societal actors as well as domestic and international institutions likely indicates *either an independence between people's support for the capital punishment restoration and their perception of EU membership conditionality helpful to democratization of Albania, or a negative association between people's support for death penalty reinstatement and their perception of EU membership conditionality being helpful to the democratization of Albania.*

Data and methods

We test our argument with a probability simple random sample of public opinion survey data that our research team collected in summer 2016 in Albania using a cellphone random digit dialling (RDD) technique through the *iziSurvey* digital platform.[97] We test four ordinal dependent variables that measured people's support for women, ethnic minority and homosexual rights, as well as support for Syrian refugees to settle in Albania (a proxy for support for refugee rights), and support for reinstatement of the death penalty in Albania. All of the variables are measured as 0 = Not at all; 1 = Little; 2 = Somewhat; and 3 = Much. Our key independent variable is respondents' beliefs that EU membership conditionality helps the country's democratisation (also measured as an ordinal response of 0 = Not at all; 1 = Little; 2 = Somewhat; and 3 = Much). We believe that our measurement of people's evaluation of EU membership conditionality is better than a more specific question of support for EU membership conditionality, which would bring issues of national sovereignty into the question context. However, we also ask respondents specifically whether or not they believe that EU membership questions the country's sovereignty (0 = Not at all; 1 = Little; 2 = Somewhat; and 3 = Much). Controlling for the latter variable helps to dissect the effect of our key independent variable, since the issue of national sovereignty continues to be a thorn in the side of the affirmation of human rights as *jus cogens* as the basic principle of international law.[98] We also control for support for the EU membership. Drawing from extant literature related to people's attitudes toward certain human rights, we control for age, gender, education, economic optimism, incomes, employment status, trust in politicians and trust in the judiciary.

It is obvious that dependent variables' values represent categories of attitude measurement rather than attitudinal fixed and exact points. It seems reasonable that lurking under the survey questions is a continuous range of unobserved attitudes and policy preferences (with real values of attitude presumably ranging from $-\infty$ to $+\infty$), normally distributed around the typical (presumably mixed) perception of the policy and tapering off such that only very few people greatly abhor or truly yearn the specified human rights. Therefore, ordered probit models would be most appropriate for this multivariate analysis of normally distributed data.

Results and discussion

We begin our statistical analysis with a frequency table of the five independent variables that we consider in this research. Tables 1 and 2 show significant differences of people's

Table 1. Frequency distribution of the dependent variables.

	Support women rights	Support minority rights	Support homosexual rights	Support Syrian refugees in Albania	Support restoration of death penalty
Not at all	15	49	674	346	344
	1.53	*5.04*	*62.69*	*36.73*	*35.87*
Little	41	100	101	165	123
	4.18	*10.28*	*10.51*	*17.52*	*12.83*
Somewhat	75	214	117	242	176
	7.65	*21.99*	*12.17*	*25.69*	*18.35*
Much	850	610	69	189	316
	86.65	*62.69*	*7.18*	*20.06*	*32.95*
Total	981	973	961	942	959

Note: Relative frequencies are in italics below frequencies.

attitudes toward the five different attitudes measured by those variables. First, there are significant differences between the three issues explicitly linked with human rights. In regards to all these issues people are inclined to take extreme stances, with the bulk of the data tending toward much support for women rights and ethnic minority rights, and the bulk of the data tending toward little support for homosexual rights. The data for the two other issues, support for Syrian refugees to settle in Albania and support for the reinstatement of the death penalty seem to be more symmetrically distributed, although many extreme stances on both tails dim the steep of the bell shaped curve, making it look more as a wave. Those findings increase our confidence that this diversity in data distribution across the five dependent variables would help our confidence in the findings (Figure 1).

Table 3 includes our five predictive models, one for each dependent variable, each of them including our key independent variables as well as control variables. Models 1, 2, 3 and 4 show a strong association between beliefs that EU membership conditionality helps the country's democratisation, whereas such an association does not appear with Model 5. This is clear evidence that people do not view support for the death penalty restoration through the same prism as the other four issues. However, support for the country's EU membership only associates with support for women rights and minority rights, but the relationship of that variable with the other dependent variables does not show any statistical significance. This is a hint that people tend to associate their support for women, ethnic minority, homosexual and refugee rights with their belief that EU membership conditionality is helping the country's democratisation rather than with their support for country's EU membership. However, there is no evidence that people associate their attitudes toward the capital punishment restoration with their belief that EU membership helps democratisation, or even support for the country's EU membership. Instead, we could see an association between support for the death penalty reinstatement and lack of trust in the judiciary. Moreover, people's view of EU membership conditionality as

Table 2. Weighted means for the dependent variables.

	Support women rights	Support minority rights	Support homosexual rights	Support Syrian refugees in Albania	Support restoration of death penalty
Mean	2.79	2.42	.58	1.26	1.37
Standard error	*.02*	*.04*	*.04*	*.04*	*.05*
Observations	981	973	961	942	959

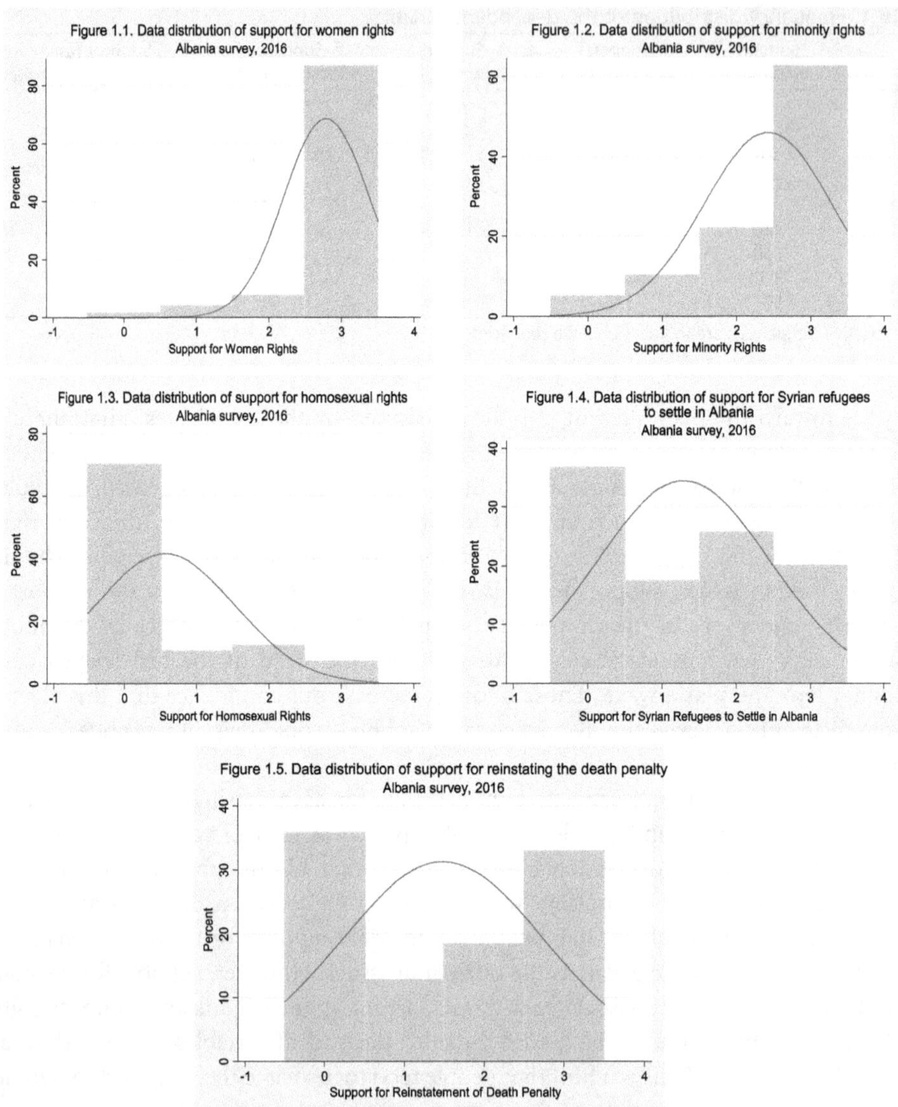

Figure 1. Visual presentation of data distribution for the dependent variables.

questioning the country's sovereignty does not seem to play any role in their attitudes toward women, ethnic minority, homosexual and refugee rights, as well as in their support for the capital punishment restoration. Clearly, whereas our respondents tend to link attitudes toward certain human rights with the EU, they also tend to view the reinstatement of the death penalty as a public policy related to their beliefs about how the judicial system in Albania works.

Conclusions

As the title of this paper suggests, EU membership conditionality can serve as an agent of human rights *jus cogens*. The latter emerged as an effort to set limits on absolute state

Table 3. Predictive models of Albanians' attitudes toward human rights.

Ordered probit Dependent variable:	MODEL 1 Support women rights	MODEL 2 Support minority rights	MODEL 3 Support homosexual rights	MODEL 4 Support Syrian refugees in Albania	MODEL 5 Support restoring death penalty
Age	−.01	−.01	−.18***	.07***	.11***
	.04	*.03*	*.03*	*.02*	*.02*
Sex	.54***	.08	.19**	−.24***	.08
	.12	*.09*	*.09*	*.08*	*.08*
Education	.04**	.02	.02	.01	−.01
	.02	*.02*	*.01*	*.01*	*.01*
Household economic trends	−.03	.14**	−.05	−.07	−.07
	.09	*.07*	*.07*	*.06*	*.06*
Personal incomes	−.03	−.01	.07***	.02	−.00
	.02	*.02*	*.02*	*.02*	*.02*
Unemployed	.04	−.22**	−.06	.16*	.02
	.14	*.10*	*.11*	*.10*	*.10*
Trust in politicians	.02	.10**	.08	.08*	−.01
	.07	*.05*	*.05*	*.05*	*.05*
Trust in judiciary	−.04	−.07	.09*	.06	−.13***
	.06	*.05*	*.05*	*.04*	*.05*
EU conditions question sovereignty	−.07	−.04	−.03	.02	.02
	.05	*.04*	*.04*	*.04*	*.04*
EU conditions help democratisation	.18***	.22***	.17***	.18***	−.01
	.06	*.05*	*.06*	*.05*	*.04*
Support country's EU membership	.14**	.11**	−.04	.05	−.01
	.04	*.05*	*.06*	*.05*	*.05*
Cutpoint 1	−1.12	−.89	.86	.79	−.21
	.35	*.27*	*.28*	*.25*	*.25*
Cutpoint 2	−.48	−.21	1.24	1.27	.13
	.39	*.26*	*.29*	*.25*	*.25*
Cutpoint 3	−.00	.52	1.87	2.05	.62
	.34	*.26*	*.29*	*.26*	*.25*
Observations	841	836	830	813	826
Preudo-R^2	.06	.04	.06	.03	.02

Note: Standard errors are reported in italics below the β coefficients.
$^{***}p < .01$, $^{**}p < .05$, $^{*}p < .1$.

sovereignty as the founding principle of international law, that is set limits in terms of the obligation of states to comply with *jus cogens* norms such that a violation would be ultra vires the state's sovereign jurisdiction. However, that scholarly exercise is highly philosophical, and could be empirically challenged. For if countries exercise their sovereignty by signing international treaties and conventions that amount to international law, how would individuals exercise their sovereign agency? Traditionally, we knew that people could do it through a social contract, which delegates individual sovereignty, at least temporarily, to the state. Now that this very state's claim to absolute sovereignty is being constrained by a higher source of a higher set of norms, wouldn't we at least make some empirical efforts toward how that presumably sovereign individual views those human rights? Since individual agency representation by one's own state is being questioned, wouldn't we at least ask that very individual what he/she wants? The Council of Europe and EU officials are quick to dismiss any suggestions for referendums on sensitive human rights issues, including abortion and capital punishment as populism.[99] However, there is always the risk that the ontological assumptions and premises of *jus cogens* will be challenged by the populace which may feel that the social contract should function the way it has worked thus far; or that in the case when the source of the international law is ultimately reliant in part on the individual's political agency, that individual should express his/her own political will through public opinion polls and referendums. We saw that our recipients appreciated the human right deliverer, EU membership conditionality, except for one case, the one related to their attitudes toward the reinstatement of the death penalty.

Our findings could be instructive for the scholarly debate on whether or not the international legal system should rely on customary law or on *jus cogens*. Whereas we refrain from taking any normative position, our findings suggest that, at least in the case of EU membership serving as an agent of human rights *jus cogens*, in Albania people tend to view the death penalty reinstatement independent of their view of its deliverer, EU membership conditionality, as a force behind democratisation. In other words, there might be discrepancies between what people consider to be (arguably human rights *jus cogens*) and what scholars and justices might philosophically include in such a category. Such a discrepancy opens up the issue that, if individual political agency is a vital source of selected human rights *jus cogens* as practiced then individuals should have the opportunity to provide input into the debate. In the name of human rights *jus cogens* and under open pressure from the EU through EU membership conditionality, the abolition of the death penalty in former communist Eastern Europe happened by explicitly excluding the masses (the community of the individuals) from the process. Other research might highlight other human rights issues where scholars and judges on the one hand and the masses on the other do not concur. However, as argued before, and also in this article, it will continue to be increasingly difficult to justify a certain policy as deriving from the principle of *jus cogens* if the very individual, who is according to a natural law analysis of human rights *jus cogens*, the source and the beneficiary of that norm, resists appropriating it as such.

Notes

1. Anthony D'Amato, 'Human Rights as Part of Customary International Law: A Plea for Change of Paradigms', *Georgia Journal of International Law* 25 (1996): 47.
2. Ridvan Peshkopia, 'The Ontology of Human Rights Socialization: The Case of Albania', in *European Institutions, Democratization, and Human Rights in the European Periphery*', ed. Henry F. Carey (Laham: Lexington Books, 2014), 337.
3. Shareen Hertel, Lyle Scruggs, and C. Patrick Heidkamp, 'Human Rights and Public Opinion: From Attitudes to Action', *Political Science Quarterly* 124 (2009): 443.
4. Brad R. Roth, 'Sovereign Equality and Non-Liberal Regime', in *Netherlands Yearbook of International Law 2012*, ed. J.E. Nijman and W.G. Werner (The Hague: T.M.C. Asser Press, 2012), 25.
5. William E. Conklin, 'The Peremptory Norms of the International Community', *The European Journal of International Law* 23 (2012): 837.
6. Ibid.; James Crawford, *The International Law Commission's Articles on State Responsibility: Introduction, Text, and Commentaries* (Cambridge, Cambridge University Press, 2002), 209.
7. Othon Anastasakis, 'The EU's Political Conditionality in the Western Balkans: Towards a More Pragmatic Approach', *Southeast European and Black Sea Studies* 8 (2008): 365.
8. Dinah Shelton, 'Are There Differentiations among Human Rights? Jus Cogens, Core Human Rights, Obligations Erga Omnes and Non-Derogability' (report presented in the UNIDEM seminar 'The Status of International Treaties on Human Rights, Coimbra', Portugal, October 7–8, 2005).

9. Predrag Zenović, 'Human Rights Enforcement via Peremptory Norms: A Challenge to State Sovereignty' (master thesis, Riga: Riga Graduate School of Law, 2012).
10. Shelton, 'Are There Differentiations among Human Rights?'
11. Ibid.
12. Ibid.; William E. Conklin, 'The Peremptory Norms of the International Community', *The European Journal of International Law* 23 (2012): 837.
13. Shelton, 'Are There Differentiations among Human Rights?'
14. Conklin, 'The Peremptory Norms of the International Community'.
15. Andrea Bianchi, 'Human Rights and the Magic of Jus Cogens', *The European Journal of International Law* 19 (2008): 491.
16. Ibid.
17. Ibid.
18. Roth, 'Sovereign Equality and Non-Liberal Regime'.
19. Preamble of Universal Declaration of Human Rights, at paragraph 1; Preambule of ICCPR, paragraph. 2: 'recognizing that these rights derive from the inherent dignity of the human person'; Shelton, 'Are There Differentiations among Human Rights?' The American Convention on Human Rights proclaims that the essential rights of man are not derived from one's being a national of a certain state, but are based upon attributes of the human personality, and ... they therefore justify international protection [...]. See American Convention on Human Rights, 22 November 1969, OASTS 36, O.A.S. Off. Rec. OEA/Ser.L/V/11.23, doc. 21, rev. 6 (1979), reprinted in 9 I.L.M. 673 (1970).
20. Zenović, 'Human Rights Enforcement via Peremptory Norms'.
21. Ibid.
22. Ibid.
23. Shelton, 'Are There Differentiations among Human Rights?'
24. Roth, 'Sovereign Equality and Non-Liberal Regime'.
25. Ibid.
26. Zenović, 'Human Rights Enforcement via Peremptory Norms'.
27. For instance, Dinah Shelton recognises that equality and non-discrimination is both sanctioned in the UN Charter and runs through the *jus cogens* prohibitions of genocide and slavery.
28. Philip Alston and J.H.H. Weiler, 'An Ever Closer Union in Need of a Human Rights Policy, The European Union and Human Rights', in *The EU and Human Rights*, ed. Philip Alston (Oxford: University Press Scholarship Online, 1999); Mark Bell, *Anti-discrimination Law and the European Union* (Oxford: Oxford University Press, 2002); Gráinne De Búrca, 'Fundamental Rights and the Reach of EC Law', *Oxford Journal of Legal Studies* 13 (1993): 283; Ulrich Everling, 'The Maastricht Judgment of the European Court and Its Significance for the Development of the European Union', *German Constitution and European Law* (1994): 1; Armin Von Bogdandy, 'The European Union as a Human Rights Organisation? Human Rights and the Core of the European Union', *Common Markets Law Review* 37 (2000): 1307; Weiler, 'Does Europe Need a Constitution? Reflections on Demos, Telos and the German Maastricht Decision', *European Law Journal* 1 (1995): 219; Williams, 'Enlargement of the Union and Human Rights Conditionality: A Policy of Distinction?' *European Law Review* 25 (2000): 601.
29. Tawhida Ahmed and Israel de Jesús Butler, 'The European Union and Human Rights: An International Law Perspective', *European Journal of International Law* 17 (2006): 771; Indrė Skersytė, 'Human Rights as Conditionality in European Union Enlargement Process' (master thesis, University of Tilburg, 2012).
30. Ahmed and Butler, 'The European Union and Human Rights'.
31. Skersytė, 'Human Rights as Conditionality'.
32. The Union is founded on the values of respect for human dignity, freedom, democracy, equality, the rule of law and respect for human rights, including the rights of persons belonging to minorities. Treaty of the European Union, Article 2.

33. Treaty of the European Union, Article 2, states: 'The Union recognizes the rights, freedoms and principles set out in the Charter of Fundamental Rights of the European Union of 7 December 2000, as adapted at Strasbourg, on 12 December 2007, which shall have the same legal value as the Treaties'.
34. Sionaidh Douglas-Scott, 'The European Union and Human Rights after the Treaty of Lisbon', *Human Rights Law Review* 11 (2011): 645.
35. However, scholars have pointed to new problem with the new human rights regime; it appears that there exists not a lack, but possibly a surfeit of human rights protection within the European legal space. A pertinent question might be whether fundamental rights are indeed 'lost in complexity'. There are now at least three possible judicial avenues for European residents to assert their human rights. First they have their national courts; secondly, if this fails, once they have exhausted domestic remedies, they may proceed in the European Court of Human Rights (ECtHR) in Strasbourg; third, if the matter is one that falls within the competence of the EU, they may have a claim under EU law, either in their national courts, in the CJEU, or both. See Douglas-Scott, 'The European Union and Human Rights'.
36. Zenović, 'Human Rights Enforcement via Peremptory Norms'.
37. Ridvan Peshkopia, *Conditioning Democratization: Institutional Reforms and EU Membership Conditionality in Albania and Macedonia* (London, New York, and Delhi: Anthem Press).
38. Othon Anastasakis and Dimitar Bechev, 'EU Conditionality in South East Europe: Bringing Commitment to the Process' (unpublished manuscript, Oxford: University of Oxford, 2003).
39. Heather Grabbe, 'A Partnership for Accession? The Implications of EU Conditionality for the Central and East European Applicants' (Robert Schuman Center Working Paper 12/99, European University Institute, 1999).
40. Heather Grabbe, 'Europeanization Goes East: Power and Uncertainty in the EU Accession Proccess', in *The Politics of Europeanization*, ed. Kevin Featherstone and Claudio M. Radaelli (Oxford: Oxford University Press, 2003), 303.
41. Andrew Moravcsik and Milada Anna Vachudova, 'The Causes and Consequences of EU Enlargement', in *The Politics of European Union Enlargement: Theoretical Approaches*, ed. Frank Schimelfenning and Ulrich Sedelmeier (London and New York: Routledge, 2005), 198; Frank Schimmelfenning, 'European Regional Organizations, Political Conditionality, and Democratic Transformation in Eastern Europe', *East European Politics and Societies* 21 (2007): 126; Martin Brusis, 'The Instrumental Use of European Union Conditionality: Regionalization in the Czech Republic and Slovakia', *East European Politics and Societies* 19 (2005): 291.
42. Geoffrey Pridham, *Building Democracy? The International Dimension of Democratization in Eastern Europe* (London: Leicester University Press, 1994); Paul J. Kubicek, *The European Union and Democratization* (London, New York: Routlegde, 2003).
43. Peshkopia, *Conditioning Democratization*; Grabbe, 'Europeanization Goes East'.
44. Petr Kopecký and Cass Mudde, 'What Has Eastern Europe Taught Us About the Democratization Literature (And Vice Versa)?' *European Journal of Political Research* 37 (2000): 517; David R. Cameron, 'The Challenges of Accession', *East European Politics and Societies* 17 (2003): 24.
45. Andrew C. Janos, Democracy and Multinationality in East Central Europe', in *Political Democracy and Ethnic Diversity in Modern European History*, ed. André W.M. Gerrits and Dirk Jan Wolffram (Stanford, CA: Stanford University Press 2005), 94.
46. Moravcsik and Vachudova, 'The Causes and Consequences of EU Enlargement'.
47. Peshkopia, *Conditioning Democratization.*
48. Peshkopia, *Conditioning Democratization*; Judith Hoffmann, 'Integrating Albania: The Role of the European Union in the Democratization Process', *Albanian Journal of Politics* 1 (2005): 56; Gregory Flynn and Henry Farrell, 'Piecing Together the Democratic Peace: The CSCE, Norms, and the "Construction" of Security in Post-Cold War Europe', *International Organization* 53 (1999): 505.

49. Ridvan Peshkopia and Arben Imami, 'Between Elite Compliance and State Socialisation: The Abolition of the Death Penalty in Eastern Europe', *The International Journal of Human Rights* 12 (2008), 353; Ridvan Peshkopia, 'The Ontology of Human Rights Socialization: The Case of Albania', in *European Institutions, Democratization, and Human Rights in the European Periphery*, ed. Henry F. Carey (Laham: Lexington Books, 2014), 337.
50. Peshkopia, 'The Ontology of Human Rights Socialization'.
51. Peshkopia and Imami, 'Between Elite Compliance and State Socialisation'.
52. Douglas-Scott, 'The European Union and Human Rights after the Treaty of Lisbon'. See also Zolkos, 'Bringing Human Rights'.
53. Peshkopia, 'The Ontology of Human Rights Socialization'.
54. Velina Lilyanova, 'Women in the Western Balkans Gender Equality in the EU Accession Process', in *Briefing* (Brussels: European Parliament, 2018).
55. Evie Browne, 'Gender in the Western Balkans' (K4D Helpdesk Report, Brighton, UK: Institute of Development Studies, 2017).
56. European Commission, 'Albania 2018 Report' (Strasbourg, 17.4.2018, SWD, 2018), 151 final, https://ec.europa.eu/neighbourhood-enlargement/sites/near/files/20180417-albania-report.pdf.
57. European Commission, 'Key Findings of the 2018 Report on Albania'.
58. European Commission, 'Albania Progress Report', October 2014, https://ec.europa.eu/neighbourhood-enlargement/sites/near/files/pdf/key_documents/2014/20141008-albania-progress-report_en.pdf.
59. European Commission, 'Key Findings of the 2018 Report on Albania', *Brussels*, April 17, 2018, http://europa.eu/rapid/press-release_MEMO-18-3403_en.htm.
60. Cecilie Endresen, 'Status Report Albania 100 Years: Symbolic Nation-Building Completed?' in *Strategies of Symbolic Nation-Building in South Eastern Europe*, ed. P. Kolstø (Furnham: Ashgate Publishers, 2014), 201; Konstantinos Giakoumis, 'Current Issues on the Protection of Minority Cultural Heritage in Albania' (paper presented at conference 'La Protection de la diversité culturelle dans le sud-est européen. Cadre juridique et réalités du terrain', Strasbourg, December 2–3, 2010). Miranda Vickers, 'The Greek Minority in Albania: Current Tensions' (Balkan Series of the Research and Assessment Branch, UK Defence Academy, 2010), http://www.voltairenet.org/IMG/pdf/Greek_minority_in_Albania.pdf.
61. Giakoumis, 'Current Issues on the Protection of Minority Cultural Heritage in Albania'.
62. Vickers, 'The Greek Minority in Albania'.
63. Ibid.
64. Ibid.
65. Ibid.; Giakoumis, 'Current Issues on the Protection of Minority Cultural Heritage in Albania'; Peshkopia, *Conditioning Democratization*.
66. Giakoumis, 'Current Issues on the Protection of Minority Cultural Heritage in Albania.'
67. Ibid.
68. Peshkopia, 'The Ontology of Human Rights Socialization'.
69. Ibid.
70. Christian K. Vinther, 'Between Liberal Policies and Conservative Values: The Role of the EU in Improving Sexual Minority Rights in Albania' (master thesis, Prague: Charles University, 2015).
71. Ben Andoni, 'Homophobia in Albania', *Gays Without Borders*, December 5, 2007, https://gayswithoutborders.wordpress.com/2007/12/05/homophobia-in-albania/.
72. Peshkopia, 'The Ontology of Human Rights Socialization'.
73. *Sot News*, '"Martesat gay", homoseksualët zbardhin tradhtinë e Ramës: Do ta ndëshkojmë' ['Gay marriages', Homosexuals Reveal Rama's Betrayal: We'll Hold him Accountable], August 14, 2016, https://sot.com.al/opinion-editorial/%E2%80%9Cmartesat-gay%E2%80%9D-homoseksual%C3%ABt-zbardhin-tradhtin%C3%AB-e-ram%C3%ABs-do-ta-nd%C3%ABshkojm%C3%AB.
74. *Panorama Online*, 'Dështon parada gay, myslimanët: Në BE me vlera, jo me homoseksualë' [Gay parade fails. Muslims: In Europe by values, not homosexuals], May 18, 2912, http://www.panorama.com.al/ambasadori-per-paraden-gay-spahia-injorante-ka-gjithandej/.

75. Rosemary Byrne, 'Future Perspectives: Accession and Asylum in an Expanded European Union', in *The New Asylum Countries? Migration Control and Refugee Protection in an Enlarged European Union*, ed. Rosemary Byrne, Gregor Noll, and J. Vedsted-Hansen (The Hague: Kluwer, 2002), 403; Liv Feijen, 'Asylum Conditionality: Development of Asylum Systems in the Western Balkans in the Context of the European Union's External Dimension', *ERA Forum* 8 (2007), 459.
76. Peshkopia, *Conditioning Democratization.*
77. Ridvan Peshkopia, 'Albania and the Balkan Route' (paper presented in the Conference on Albanian Societies in Transition, December 19–20, 2008, New York).
78. John Morrison and Beth Crosland, 'The Trafficking and Smuggling of Refugees: The End Game in European Asylum Policy?' (working paper no. 39, New Issues in Refugee Research, UNHCR, 2001).
79. Sandra Lavenex, 'Asylum, Immigration and Central-Eastern Europe: Challenges to EU Enlargement', *European Foreign Affairs Review* 3 (1998): 275; Stephan Anagnost, 'Challenges Facing Asylum System and Asylum Policy Development in Europe: Preliminary Lessons Learned from Central European and Baltic States (CEBS)', *International Journal of Refugee Law* 12 (2000): 280.
80. Kosta Barjaba and Russell King, 'Introducing and Theorizing Albanian Migration', in *The New Albanian Migration*, ed. Russell King, Nicola Mai, and Stephanie Schwandner-Sievers (Brighton: Sussex Academic Press, 2005), 1.
81. INSTAT. Popullsia e Shqipërisë, 1 Janar 2018 [Population of Albania, 1 January 2018], http://www.instat.gov.al/al/temat/treguesit-demografik%C3%AB-dhe-social%C3%AB/popullsia/publikimet/2018/popullsia-e-shqip%C3%ABris%C3%AB-1-janar-2018/. INSTAT Migracioni në Shqipëri, Maj 2014 [Migration in Albania, May 2014], http://www.instat.gov.al/media/3078/migracioni_ne_shqiperi.pdf.
82. Joana Hanson, 'Kosovo Albanian Refugees: Perceptions of the Motherland', *The RUSI Journal* 146 (2001): 28.
83. Gjergj Erebara, 'Albania Would Welcome Refugees, Rama Says', *BalkanInsight*, September 16, 2015.
84. Peshkopia, *Conditioning Democratization.*
85. Myria Georgiou and Rafal Zaborowski, 'Media Coverage of the "Refugee Crisis": A Cross-European Perspective' (council of Europe report, Strasbourg: Council of Europe, 2017).
86. Leonard Ray, 'When Parties Matter: The Conditional Influence of Party Positions on Voter Opinions about European Integration', *The Journal of Politics* 65 (2003): 978.
87. Carolyn Smith Keller, 'Perceived Immigrant Threat: On the Gender Difference among Political Elites', in *National and European? Polish Political Elite in Comparative Perspective*, ed. Wlodzimierz Weselowski, Kazimierz M. Slomczynski, and Joshua Kjerulf Dubrow (Warsaw: IFiS Publishers, 2011).
88. Ridvan Peshkopia and Arben Imami, 'Between Elite Compliance and State Socialisation: The Abolition of the Death Penalty in Eastern Europe', *The International Journal of Human Rights* 12 (2008): 353.
89. Ibid.
90. Ibid.
91. Giorgio Malinverni and Hanna Suchocka, 'Opinion on the Compatibility of the Death Penalty with the Constitution of Albania', http://www.venice.coe.int/docs/1999/CDL(1999)001-e.asp.
92. Peshkopia and Imami, 'Between Elite Compliance and State Socialisation'.
93. Ibid.
94. See for instance, Bota Sot, '"Dënim me vdekje për kriminelët", të afërm të viktimave kërkojnë kthimin e denimit kapital' ["Death penalty for criminels", relatives of the victims demand the restoration of capital punishment], August 13, 2018, https://www.botasot.info/shqiperia/935262/denim-me-vdekje-per-kriminelet-te-aferm-te-viktimave-kerkojne-kthimin-e-denimit-kapital/.
95. *Ora News*, 'Basha i gatshëm të mbajë referendum për kthimin e dënimit me vdekje' [Opposition leader] Basha ready to hold a referendum on the reinstatement of the death penalty], October 13, 2018, http://www.oranews.tv/article/basha-i-gatshem-te-mbaje-referendum-

kthimin-e-denimit-me-vdekje; *Tema Online*, 'Saimir Tahiri u përgjigjet komentuesve që kërkojnë rikthimin e dënimit me vdekje' [Minister of the Interior] Saimir Tahiri addresses commentators who seek the death penalty restoration], July 7, 2015, http://www.gazetatema.net/2015/07/07/tahiri-iu-pergjigjet-komentuesve-qe-kerkojne-rikthimin-e-denimit-me-vdekje/.

96. *Ora News*, 'Basha Ready to Hold a Referendum on the Reinstatement of the Death Penalty'.
97. For a more detailed description of data collection methodology, questions asked and variable values, please contact the first author.
98. Zenović, 'Human Rights Enforcement via Peremptory Norms'; Roth, 'Sovereign Equality and non-Liberal Regime'. D'Amato, 'Human Rights as Part of Customary International Law'.
99. Peshkopia and Imami, 'Between Elite Compliance and State Socialisation'.

Acknowledgment

We are grateful to Sonja Grover for her patience with us during our process of preparing the manuscript for this special issue. Also, we are grateful to our colleagues who worked with collecting the data, namely Habibe Ademi, Teuta Agushi, Liri Kosovare Bllaca, Bujeta Buja, Saranda Fazliu, Erjon Fejzullahu, Shpëtim Kadriu, Erza Kqiku, Ridvan Marevci, Shkëlqim Mehmeti, Shkelzen Musliu, Ariana Orllati, Shëndriza Prokshi, Arbenita Qeriqi, Shqipdona Reshani, Valdet Rexhepi, Samire Sadiku, Elma Salihu, Erza Salihu, Berta Sopa, Gresa Sheqiri, Anduena Zeka, Blerina Zeqiri, and Antoneta Zhjeqi. A special gratitude goes to Eno Minka of the Vodafone Albania who helped us with technical issues during the survey process.

Disclosure statement

No potential conflict of interest was reported by the authors.

Index

For Product Safety Concerns and Information please contact our EU
representative GPSR@taylorandfrancis.com
Taylor & Francis Verlag GmbH, Kaufingerstraße 24, 80331 München, Germany

www.ingramcontent.com/pod-product-compliance
Lightning Source LLC
LaVergne TN
LVHW080658011026
849160LV00014B/1466

* 9 7 8 1 0 3 2 0 8 4 0 6 0 *